THE DRIVE METHOD

HOW TO MAKE ENGAGEMENT SURVIVE WHEN REWARDS STOP

A great performance isn't a lucky accident. It's the result one gets when human nature meets favourable circumstances. By aligning organizational systems with how human motivation actually works, companies can transform engagement, unlocking unprecedented levels of creativity, problem-solving, and innovation.

I dedicate this book to people who are passionate about creating great companies and products and bringing out the best in people, in harmony with human nature. They know that these goals are symbiotic. This book is for you.

CONTENTS

PART III. EXECUTION

DRIVE METHOD™: A ROADMAP TO MOTIVATION THAT LASTS . . . 99

NOW EXECUTE 151

INTRODUCTION

Let's leave the usual platitudes aside. This isn't a book about "finding your why," nor is it a manifesto for the gamification-obsessed or a rallying cry to abandon KPIs. Instead, think of it as a guide for the curious leader, someone who suspects that the real levers of human performance are hidden in plain sight, buried beneath layers of management dogma and motivational folklore.

We've spent decades treating motivation as a question of carrot and stick, of bonuses and badges, as if people were slot machines waiting for the right combination of incentives. But what if the real secret to unlocking creativity, engagement, and innovation lies not in what we dangle in front of people, but in the invisible architecture of the systems we build around them? What if, instead of trying to "motivate" people, we simply stopped demotivating them?

This book is an invitation to look at your organization through a new lens. A lens informed by behavioral science, evolutionary biology, and the messy, glorious reality of human nature. It's about designing environments where people don't just comply, but commit; where performance isn't extracted, but emerges. If you're ready to challenge the status quo and build something that actually works for humans, not just for spreadsheets, read on.

Hi I'm Roman, your author of this book.

If you had asked my teachers back in the day, I was the quintessential troublemaker. I had a knack for distracting others, staying focused in class was nearly impossible, and I'd jump at any chance to divert my attention elsewhere. The worst part for me? Memorization. Vocabulary lists were a nightmare, and sitting still for hours felt like an impossible task. Their assessment was spot-on when it came to school, but it only applied to the classroom. Unfortunately, I only realized this much later.

Because in other areas of my life, things looked completely different. My hobbies? I could sit there for hours, and completely immerse myself in building aircraft models, inventing stories for pen&paper games or any other challenge that came my way. And in sports? I was focused, relentless, and unwilling take the easy way. In-depth learning on topics that sparked my curiosity? I could go on for hours.

It was a stark contrast to the restlessness and distraction I experienced in school.

And here's the thing: I know I'm not alone in this. We struggle to concentrate in one context but can become utterly engrossed in another. The fascinating part for me was realizing that my inability to focus in school wasn't about my intelligence or abilities. Clearly, I had the capacity for deep concentration and effort, but only under the right circumstances.

So, I started to ask myself: what makes one context easy to engage in, while another feels like torture? What's going on when we can focus on our interests for hours, but struggle with something else for minutes? As I looked around, I saw this wasn't just my experience; it's universal. Men, women, children. People from all walks of life share this phenomenon. What is the common thread? We're all human, shaped by evolution, with consistent neurochemical foundations that govern our behavior.

That's where my journey began. The search for answers to two questions:

What makes something enjoyable just for the sake of doing it? How do you trigger intrinsic motivation?

Over the years I've learned that the key is not as much about personality as you might think. No, a huge part of the answer lies in our biology, specifically our shared neurochemistry. And that's what led me to another fundamental question: What is the scientific formula for intrinsic motivation? That kind of motivation that seems to be most effective to reach something known as cognitive peak performance.

It's a question that has driven me ever since, and it's the reason behind everything in this book: the search business process designs that unlocks intrinsic motivation.

What I believe

For as long as businesses, educators, and leaders have sought to unlock the full potential of human performance, one myth has persisted: that human behavior is unpredictable, driven by fleeting emotions, external pressures, and unknown complexities. This has led to decades of trial-and-error approaches, motivational fads, and a (often) misplaced reliance on extrinsic rewards like bonuses, points, or accolades.

But what if the answers were always within reach? What if the mystery of human behavior and with it of human motivation could be better understood by looking at something deeper, something fundamental, something coded into the very fabric of who we are?

Here's my point: human behavior isn't totally random, nor is it a puzzle with infinite pieces. It is complex, true, and to a degree that it cannot be truly predicted. But it also follows laws as old and enduring as life itself. These laws have been shaped by millions of years of evolution, encoded into our biology to ensure our survival. The same instincts that drove our ancestors to explore, collaborate and innovate in the wild, now drive us to solve problems, master skills, and connect with others in the modern classroom, workplace, and beyond.

This book is built on one profound realization: **human behavior and its motivation is more predictable than most of us believe.** Especially if you understand its evolutionary roots. While the details of daily life, the small wins, the setbacks, the micro-trends may fluctuate, the macro-trend of human behavior is consistent and reliable. Beneath the noise of day-to-day variability lies a clear signal: people have a desire to perform. Not a management-goals-driven KPI performance, but performance that lets our species experience progress. Crazy enough, even 'almost-there-progress'.[1][2]

We all know this from our own experiences performing sports, hobbies, or playing games. Not coincidentally within these activities people are also challenged meaningfully, given autonomy, supported in mastery, encouraged to collaborate and free to explore. Over the next pages, we will analyze how these factors form the building blocks of the powerful drive known as intrinsic motivation.

Info Box: What is Intrinsic Motivation?

Intrinsic motivation refers to doing something because it is inherently interesting, enjoyable, or meaningful rather than because of external pressures or rewards. When we act out of intrinsic motivation, the activity itself is the reward. Think of losing track of time while working on a hobby, solving a tough puzzle, or learning a new skill purely out of curiosity.

How I See Intrinsic Motivation

To me, intrinsic motivation is the psychological engine that powers our best work and deepest learning. It's what pulls us into a state of flow[3], where effort feels almost effortless, and we're energized by the challenge itself. It's the difference between "having to" and "wanting to." In my experience, environments that support autonomy, mastery, and progress naturally foster intrinsic motivation. There, people don't need to be pushed; they lean in because they want to.

How Is It Different from Extrinsic Motivation?

Extrinsic motivation, by contrast, is driven by external rewards (like money, grades, bonuses, or praise) or the avoidance of negative consequences (like punishment or criticism). It's about doing something to get something else. While extrinsic motivators can be effective for routine or short-term tasks, they rarely spark the kind of engagement, creativity, or resilience that comes from being intrinsically motivated.

In short:

Intrinsic motivation = Doing something because you find it interesting, meaningful, or enjoyable.

Extrinsic motivation = Doing something to earn a reward or avoid punishment.

Understanding this distinction is crucial: systems built only on extrinsic motivators often backfire in the long run, while those that cultivate intrinsic motivation unlock deeper, more sustainable engagement and performance.

For me, this realization isn't just empowering, it's revolutionary. It tells us that building organizations, teams, and systems around motivated behavior does not need to be a gamble or a guess. It's a strategy rooted in nature's blueprint. And when we align with this blueprint, we create environments where people don't just perform, but are able to thrive.

In the following pages, we want to dispel a few myths (Part 1), replace them with current and proven insights (Part 2) and enable you to apply this knowledge in practice by providing you with my own tested tools (Part 3).

It isn't about adding just another tool to your management toolbox or checking off a list of engagement strategies. It's about understanding the core of what makes us human and designing experiences, systems, and cultures that resonate with our deepest instincts.

The implications are profound:

- Imagine a workplace where people don't need to be pushed to perform, but they are naturally pulled by the desire to grow, solve, and contribute.

- Imagine teams that don't just comply with instructions, but innovate and adapt because their curiosity and creativity are fully engaged.

- Imagine a world where leadership isn't about control, but about creating the conditions where people's intrinsic motivation flourishes.

It's about designing systems that align with human nature in a way that is sustainable, ethical, and profoundly impactful.

And here's the best part: this isn't just theory. The laws of motivation have already been tested, refined, and proven by evolution itself. Our ancestors didn't survive just by chasing external rewards or avoiding punishment. They advanced because they were curious, driven to master their environment, and motivated to collaborate and explore.

I will show you how to apply these timeless principles to modern challenges. It will give you the tools to design for intrinsic motivation in your organization, your team, or even your personal life. By the time you finish reading, you'll see that the path to motivation, engagement, and fulfillment isn't hidden or elusive. It's as natural, and as inevitable, as growth itself.

So, as you turn the page, ask yourself: What would be possible if you aligned with the blueprint of human nature? What could you build if you understood not just how people behave, but why?

The answers are waiting. Let's begin.

PART
ONE

THE INDUSTRIAL-AGE HANGOVER

There's a subtle decline running through modern organizations. It's not a lack of talent. It's not poor hiring. It's not even weak leadership. The real problem is that most companies still operate with systems designed for a different century.

Performance management today is built on assumptions from the industrial age: external pressure, rigid structures, and short-term KPIs. These worked when efficiency meant how fast a person could tighten bolts on an assembly line. But in a world where creativity, problem-solving, and adaptability are the true currency of success, these old tools do more harm than good.[4]

For a long time, success was simply synonymous with output. More units produced. More boxes checked. More hours worked. The relationship between effort and results was linear and predictable. But in today's knowledge economy, the equation has changed. You cannot grind out innovation like you grind out widgets. Doubling someone's hours will not double their insight. The model no longer fits the task.

Still, organizations continue to assume the issue lies in their people. They chase talent, invest in training, roll out new tools, and double down on goals. They invest all of this effort, while keeping the same outdated operating system in place.

Here is the hard truth: you cannot achieve 21st-century performance with 20th-century systems. The hangover from the industrial age is real. And it is still dictating how companies try to manage human potential.

Without a System, Performance is Coincidence

Ask any leader what drives great performance and you will hear the same familiar answers. Talent. Experience. Motivation. But ask how they ensure performance happens consistently, not just during crunch time or under pressure, but predictably and sustainably. That's when the conversation dries up.

Because most companies don't have a system for this. They assume high performance just happens if they hire the right people and set the right targets. But that is like expecting

Olympic-level results without training plans, recovery cycles, or professional coaching.

We do not manage athletes this way. We do not expect elite physical performance to emerge by accident. And yet we expect knowledge workers to deliver mental excellence without rhythm, feedback, or environmental support. It is a contradiction that would be laughable if it were not so damaging.

Consider elite athletes. They don't just train harder. They train smarter. They manage nutrition, sleep, intensity, feedback, recovery, and psychological readiness. Every variable is structured. Nothing is left to chance. But in the workplace, we leave cognitive performance to luck. We hope for flashes of brilliance and occasional flow states while offering none of the conditions required to make them possible.

That is not a strategy. That is simply the principle of hope.

High performance is not magic. It is not a mystery. And it is definitely not luck. It is system design. Just like a high-performance engine needs precise tuning to run well, cognitive work requires psychological conditions that support energy, clarity, and intrinsic drive. Without those conditions, even your best people will struggle.

The Cost of Getting This Wrong

The data is unambiguous. According to Gallup, eighty-five percent of employees globally are disengaged or actively disengaged.[5] This translates to roughly seven trillion dollars in lost productivity. That is the visible cost. The invisible costs run even deeper.

Let's put to rest the tired old myth that disengagement is simply a matter of individual laziness. In reality, disengagement is what happens when you take a perfectly capable human being and drop them into a system designed to throttle autonomy, stifle mastery, and drain meaning from their work. Strip away these essential nutrients and, unsurprisingly, motivation shrivels, energy evaporates, and creativity becomes a distant memory. The best people will look for other opportunities; the rest will stay unmotivated. It's not that people don't want to perform - most are desperate to - but if the system is broken, no amount of pep talks or perks will bring them back to life. The real tragedy isn't that people lose their spark; it's that we built workplaces that snuff it out by design.

The effects compound. Innovation slows. Quality erodes. Customers notice. Culture decays. Cynicism becomes the norm. Engagement plummets. Leaders react by pushing harder, setting tighter controls, and issuing louder calls for accountability. All the while, they never question the system itself.

This cycle is not just inefficient. It is tragic. Because people want to perform. They want to solve problems, contribute meaningfully, and be proud of what they create.

You yourself are the best proof

Look closely at where people willingly give their best performance: not just at work, but in games, sports, and hobbies. Here, there are no paychecks, no quarterly reviews, yet people devote countless hours, chase improvement, and persist through setbacks. Why? Because these activities are designed to provide exactly what our brains crave: visible progress, meaningful challenge, autonomy to choose our path, opportunities for mastery, and a sense of belonging or contribution.

In sports, we train for years to shave seconds off a personal best. In games, we replay the same level a dozen times just to "almost" win. In our hobbies, we tinker, build, and refine. Not for a medal, but for the satisfaction of seeing ourselves improve. The effort feels worth it because the structure of the activity itself is rewarding.

This is not a coincidence. It's a blueprint for motivation. The very things that make games, sports, and hobbies so engaging - clear feedback, escalating challenge, autonomy, and social connection - are the same ingredients missing from so many workplaces. When organizations design with these principles in mind, performance stops being a struggle. It becomes something people seek out, not something they're forced to deliver.

But if the environment makes that impossible, the best intentions go to waste. What could have been extraordinary becomes average. Or worse.

And the irony is that all of it is avoidable.

From Hangover to Breakthrough

This is the shift we need to make. Performance is not a trait. It is an outcome. And that outcome depends entirely on how well the environment supports the way human beings actually function.

We already know what that requires. The brain has limits. Attention, focus, and decision-making all consume energy. These resources need replenishment, not just more pressure. Motivation is not summoned through willpower. It is mediated by neurochemistry. Flow states do not appear by accident. They emerge under specific conditions. Stress can be catalytic or destructive depending on how it is handled. And collaboration either amplifies thinking or shuts it down, depending on the psychological safety of the environment.

None of this is speculation. It is science. We have decades of data from neuroscience, evolutionary biology, and behavioral psychology. We know what the brain needs to perform. The problem is not lack of insight. The problem is lack of application.[6] [7]

organizations keep trying to inspire better results through slogans and superficial changes. But what they really need is system design rooted in how humans actually work. That is the difference between hoping for excellence and engineering it. Between talent drain and talent activation. Between random brilliance and repeatable performance.

To fix this, we need to go deeper than techniques and beyond motivational soundbites. We need to understand the biology of motivation.

Because once we understand how the brain generates focus, drive, and resilience, we can stop guessing. We can stop treating human performance like a roll of the dice, and we can start building environments where people naturally do their best work.

"Dopamine is a molecule in the brain and body that is closely linked to our sense of motivation. It can also enhance our depth of focus and lower our threshold for taking action toward specific goals... Dopamine is about wanting, not about having."

DR. ANDREW HUBERMAN, HUBERMAN LAB NEWSLETTER: TOOLS TO MANAGE DOPAMINE AND IMPROVE MOTIVATION & DRIVE

The Biology of Motivation

Behind every engagement strategy and performance initiative lies an invisible set of assumptions about what drives human behavior. These assumptions are often inherited from tradition, built on gut feelings, or shaped by outdated theories of behavior. And yet, they form the foundation of how we try to manage, motivate, and lead.

The problem is that many of these assumptions contradict how motivation actually works at a biological level. When our strategies run against the grain of how the human brain functions, the result is not just inefficiency. It is active resistance, disengagement, and wasted potential.

If we want to build systems that support sustained performance, creativity, and engagement, we need to move past intuition and into biology. Because human motivation is not a mystery. It is a set of patterns, mechanisms, and responses hardwired into the nervous system. When we understand those patterns, we can design environments that do not fight human nature but amplify it.

Let's begin with a basic truth. Motivation is not a single force. It is not a switch that can be flipped on or off. Motivation is a dynamic system, driven by a cocktail of neurochemicals and evolutionary adaptations. Among the most important of these are four familiar names.

- **Dopamine** drives pursuit, anticipation, and goal-directed behavior, not just the pleasure of reward.[8]
- **Serotonin** is linked to status, pride, and the sense of being valued.
- **Oxytocin** governs trust, bonding, and social connection.
- **Endorphins** reinforce effort and help us push through discomfort.

Info Box: Oxytocin & Vasopressin

When we talk about social bonding, you may have heard of oxytocin, the so-called "cuddle hormone" associated with trust, empathy, and connection. But there is another, less known, key player: vasopressin. As Robert Sapolsky and other neuroscientists have highlighted, vasopressin is crucial for loyalty, territoriality, and group defense. It is especially influential in contexts that demand cohesion under stress. Think of soldiers, sports teams, or any group facing an outside threat.

Here is the helpful nuance. Both systems exist in both sexes. The key idea is that the two chemicals are tuned somewhat differently across sexes. This shapes which situations feel especially bonding.

Put simply, oxytocin is more likely to bind people through warmth, caregiving, and face-to-face affiliation. Vasopressin is more likely to bind people through shared challenge, duty, vigilance, and protection. Because men tend to rely more on vasopressin pathways and women often show stronger oxytocin tone in at least some contexts, men may bond more readily in situations that involve coordinated effort under pressure, while women may bond more readily in settings rich in trust, care, and emotional attunement. Both routes matter for everyone, and both can be designed for.[9]

If you want to design environments or systems that foster real commitment and group loyalty, especially in male-dominated teams or high-pressure situations, do not focus only on "warm and fuzzy." Add vasopressin-relevant ingredients like shared goals under load, clear roles, earned trust through performance, and rituals of protection and duty. In mixed or female-leaning settings, include strong oxytocin cues as well. Use reliable social support, prosocial touch norms where appropriate, eye contact, and cooperative problem solving. The practical takeaway is to mix conditions that trigger both systems so diverse teams can bond through multiple channels.

This nuance is critically important for leaders designing systems for diverse teams in competitive or high-stakes environments. It cautions against a simplistic "more bonding is always better" approach. Aim instead for situational fit. Some moments call for warmth. Others call for shared strain. The best designs alternate and integrate both. For more, see Sapolsky's Behave and his lectures on the neurobiology of social bonding.

Note: Human data on receptor densities are still evolving. Many findings come from animal models and human imaging or genetic proxies. Treat the sex-difference patterns as tendencies with lots of overlap, not absolutes.

These neurochemical systems are not abstract concepts; they concretely explain the difference between environments where people come alive and those where they shut down.

What This Means for Designing Work

Science leads us to five key insights.

First, progress is more than productivity. Every time someone makes visible progress on something that matters, dopamine fires. Momentum feels good because it is biologically rewarding. This is why just enough challenge is more engaging than ease. The work feels meaningful, because it signals growth.[10]

Second, we are wired to connect. When people feel seen, trusted, and included, their brains release chemicals like serotonin and oxytocin. This is not about being nice. It is about fueling collaboration, engagement, and cognitive sharpness. Isolation and invisibility do the opposite.[11]

Third, flow is not magic. It is designable. Flow arises when a task is just hard enough to challenge us, but not so hard that it overwhelms. It depends on clear goals, fast feedback, and deep focus. When these ingredients are in place, a cascade of dopamine, endorphins, and with it focused attention follows.[12]

Fourth, autonomy is not optional. When people feel coerced, the brain triggers a threat response. Cortisol rises. Creativity and problem-solving shut down. But when people feel control over how they work, even under constraints, motivation increases. Autonomy is not a management style. It is a neuro-biological requirement.[13]

And fifth, purpose is a multiplier. When people feel that their work matters, several systems activate at once. Dopamine from progress. Serotonin from significance. Oxytocin from contribution. That is what makes meaningful work so powerful. It lights up the entire motivational system.[14]

Why Most Systems Still Fail

Most performance systems ignore these mechanisms entirely. They emphasize external control rather than internal activation. They rely on delayed rewards that are too far removed from the effort. They offer recognition in impersonal formats that do not register emotionally. They separate people instead of connecting them. And worst of all, they remove visibility from progress by focusing on outcomes solely.

Even well-meaning initiatives can backfire. If the system fails to support autonomy, feedback, or trust, it activates cortisol instead of dopamine. It suppresses motivation rather than enabling it.

And while these neurochemical systems are universal, people experience them differently. Some are more driven by novelty and progress. Others respond more strongly to connection or social validation. Good systems do not flatten these differences. They make room for them.

Attention: The Missing Currency of Performance

To truly apply this knowledge, we must talk about attention. In today's economy, attention is not just a personal capacity. It is a strategic resource. It determines the quality of thinking, the depth of problem-solving, and the sharpness of creativity.

Yet most organizations treat attention as if it were limitless. They expect people to switch tasks constantly, remain accessible at all times, and maintain focus regardless of noise, stress, or fatigue. This is not just unrealistic. It is wasteful.

Attention is limited. Most people can only maintain deep focus for four to five hours a day.[15] After that, cognitive performance declines. More hours do not equal better output.

Attention is fragile. It is easily disrupted by both external triggers like interruptions and internal states like anxiety or distraction. Once broken, it takes over twenty minutes to fully return to the original task.[16]

Attention is variable. It fluctuates based on sleep, stress, emotional load, and time of day. This means peak performance cannot be scheduled arbitrarily. It must be protected and supported.

And, last but not least, attention determines value. Modern work is not about how long someone worked on a task. Nowadays, what counts is how deeply you have thought about it. An hour of high-quality attention can produce more value than an entire day of scattered effort.

When we waste attention, we waste our most valuable resource. And we do this all the time. We overload calendars. We fragment focus. We praise activity instead of insight. This is the hidden tax most organizations are paying without realizing it.

From Biology to Blueprint

So now we know a little bit more about what drives motivation. We understand more about the brain's signals for progress, connection, and autonomy. But understanding is not enough.

Knowing is not designing.

This is where struggle happens. People read the research. They recognize the problem. But when it comes to applying these insights to their own systems, they fall back on what they know. They add bonuses, create recognition programs, and roll out new communication platforms.

The result is a patchwork. A set of motivational tools bolted onto legacy structures. These systems may look modern, but they still operate on old logic. They are built to comply, not to engage.

So the real question is this. How do we take everything we now know about neurobiology and motivation and turn it into a system that actually works? Where do we find a practical architecture that builds these principles into everyday work?

Surprisingly, the answer is not in HR manuals or leadership frameworks. It is not in neuroscience keynotes or motivational posters. The most effective system for embedding intrinsic motivation into daily experience comes from an unexpected place.

Leisure activities.

And that is where we go next.

From Theory to System: Why Intrinsic Motivation Is (Often) the Missing Link

Imagine this: You have just decoded the biological foundations of motivation. You understand what triggers dopamine. You know how to shape environments that support flow. You see how autonomy, mastery, and purpose operate as a psychological symphony.

But now what?

This is the point where most organizations stall. They grasp the principles, but they cannot translate them into real systems. So they default to what they know. They offer bonuses. They launch wellness programs. They introduce new feedback platforms. But these are not design solutions. They are surface tools built for compliance, not for sustained performance.

Here is the hard truth. Most performance systems are not actually systems. They are bolt-ons. Reactive measures, loosely stitched onto legacy workflows. They aim to nudge behavior, but rarely engage motivation. They are fragmented, extrinsic, and structurally misaligned with how people actually function.

So the real question becomes this:

Where can we find a system that already runs on intrinsic drivers? One that is structured, tested, and repeatable?

The answer is not in leadership models. Not in self-help seminars. Not in another neuroscience keynote or digital transformation sprint.

The answer comes from a direction that few managers consider.

A discipline that was branded in a new way, but relies on context as old as humanity. It is an evolutionary echo that will stay with us:

Gamification. At least a particular type of it.

The Misunderstood System in Modern Psychology

This is where we must introduce a crucial distinction. We are not talking about the superficial 'points-and-badges' version of gamification. We are talking about something deeper, an approach I call **'Non-Skinnerian Gamification.'** Simply put, it's about designing systems that tap into our natural, internal drivers, like progress and mastery, rather than just 'skinning' a task with external rewards.

It is not about adding points, but activating progress.

Here is what this kind of gamification looks like:

- Progression systems that show people they are getting closer, moment by moment.

- Feedback loops that spark curiosity and support self-regulation.

- Challenge structures that push right to the edge of ability without breaking it.

- Social mechanics that support identity, belonging, and contribution.

- Autonomy systems that restore control to the individual.

These elements are not playful gimmicks. They are primal mechanisms. They mirror the way humans evolved to engage with their environment. And that is why they work. Although the term gamification is implying it, you can observe these mechanisms not only while playing games but actually in all kinds of leisure activities.

Info Box: What I Mean by Non-Skinnerian Gamification

To understand the term **Non-Skinnerian Gamification**, it helps to start with the work of B. F. Skinner. Skinner was one of the most influential psychologists of the twentieth century. His research on operant conditioning shaped the way we understand behavior, learning, and habit formation. Much of today's thinking around behavior change, reinforcement, and external motivation finds its roots in his work. For that foundational contribution, I have deep respect and gratitude.

However, Skinner's approach was developed in a different era, with different challenges in mind. His model focused primarily on observable behavior and external reinforcement. The core idea was that behavior can be shaped by systematically applying rewards or punishments. This thinking gave rise to many of the methods still found in traditional performance systems: incentive programs, point-based rewards, badges, and strict rule-based behavior control.

This legacy is still very much alive in what is commonly called gamification today. Most gamification platforms and designers continue to rely heavily on points, badges, leaderboards, levels, and prizes. These are essentially external motivators in new packaging. They follow the same Skinnerian logic: stimulate behavior through visible rewards, reinforce compliance, and try to maintain engagement by escalating extrinsic incentives.

This is exactly why I make a clear distinction.

I use the term Non-Skinnerian Gamification to separate our approach from this model. What I offer is not a reward layer. It is not about "making work fun." It is a design method that starts with intrinsic motivation and builds systems that respect how humans are wired to learn, grow, and perform.

This is not a dismissal of Skinner's legacy. In fact, it builds on it. But it also recognizes what Skinner's model could not fully explain at the time: the role of meaning, identity, curiosity, autonomy, and purpose in human motivation. It acknowledges that people are not just shaped by external consequences, but also by how they perceive challenges, how they engage with uncertainty, and how they value personal progress.

Non-Skinnerian Gamification represents a shift. It moves from external control to internal enablement. It integrates decades of insight from neuroscience, self-determination theory, evolutionary psychology, and cognitive science. It focuses not just on what people do, but why they do it, and how systems can create the right conditions for that motivation to thrive.

I use this term to draw a clear line between persuasion and empowerment. Not because I reject the past, but because the future demands another path forward. One that works with human nature, not against it.

Games Were the First Performance Systems

Thousands of years before the MBA, people designed games. Not to kill time, but to build mastery, forge bonds, and rehearse for real life.

Games are not distractions. They are compressed learning environments. They teach through feedback. They accelerate competence. They reward growth. And they do all of this without requiring money, managers, or formal instruction.

This is why someone will spend hundreds of hours solving difficult problems, collaborating with strangers, and learning complex systems inside a game. Not because someone told them to. Not because there is a paycheck. But because the design itself pulls them in.

What other system does that?

A Design Language for Motivation

When used correctly, the method in this book is not a technique. It is a design language. It turns theory into practice.

Where behavioral science tells us that people are driven by progress, purpose, and control, the tools introduced in this book build environments that make those drivers tangible.

Where psychology explains the role of identity in behavior, non-Skinnerian Gamification gives people roles, narratives, and feedback systems that reinforce who they are becoming.

Where most organizations struggle to make motivation systematic, this book provides the blueprint.

This is what makes it powerful. It does not try to force motivation from the outside. It creates conditions where motivation emerges from within.

Why It Matters Now

Work has changed. Performance is no longer about following instructions. It is about solving problems, adapting in real time, and creating new value.

In this world, intrinsic design should not be optional. It is essential. Not as a cosmetic layer on top of work, but as a framework for building work from the inside out.

We know the science behind intrinsic motivation. We know the principles. What we need is a delivery system.

What I'm going to reveal to you in this book is that system.

It is time to reclaim knowledge behind human motivation. To strip away the misunderstandings. To stop thinking of it as a novelty and start seeing it for what it truly is:

The most scalable, flexible, and biologically aligned system we have for enabling peak human performance.

And that is where we go next. We will rebuild it from the ground up.

PART
TWO

CONTEXT

Challenging Common Misconceptions About Gamification's Role in Motivation

The moment we introduce the topic of *gamification*, something happens. People either light up with excitement or shut down with skepticism. Some imagine playful engagement, others picture gimmicks and manipulation. Most assume it has something to do with points, badges, leaderboards, or digital tools that "make work fun."

This confusion is not accidental. It reflects how gamification has been misunderstood, misapplied, and commercialized over the past decade. What began as a serious attempt to improve motivation design quickly devolved into surface-level techniques that treat behavior like a slot machine.

So let us start by clearing the air.

Gamification, in its original intent, was never about adding games to work. It was about applying the principles that make games deeply engaging, challenging, and meaningful to real-world systems. It was about bringing the mechanics of progress, feedback, exploration, and mastery into environments where those qualities are often missing.[17]

Unfortunately, the business world embraced only the most visible elements. Points. Badges. Leaderboards. The thinking was simple: if games motivate people, then we just need to copy what games look like.

But what makes games motivating is not what they look like. It is how they are designed.

People do not spend hours immersed in a game because of the reward at the end. They stay because of the journey. Because they are learning. Because they are overcoming meaningful challenges subjectively. Because they can see progress, feel growth, and act independently..

When companies reduce gamification to reward mechanisms, they miss the point entirely. Instead of activating intrinsic motivation, they reinforce the very dynamics that weaken it. They replace thoughtful design with superficial features and call it engagement.

This is why we challenge the common view.

Gamification is not about manipulation. It is about architecture. It is not about tricking people into doing things, but creating environments where people want to engage, learn, and contribute.

The most effective gamification does not try to control behavior. It creates conditions where behavior becomes self-directed. It helps people feel progress without needing external praise. It transforms systems that drain motivation into systems that generate it.

In truth, the only reason gamification has a bad reputation is because most of what is called gamification is not really gamification.

That is why we (have to) use a different term. **Non-Skinnerian Gamification** marks a departure from reward-driven behaviorism and points toward something deeper. It signals a commitment to motivation that is designed for human performance, not just short-term compliance.

So if you have dismissed gamification in the past, we understand. The version you saw probably even deserved it. But what you are about to see is something very different.

Quick examples:

The Fitness Tracker Trap

Consider two apps designed to help people get more active.

App A tracks your steps, gives you badges for daily goals, ranks you on a leaderboard, and sends push notifications when you fall behind others. It works well. At first. People behave. They compete. Engagement spikes. But after a few weeks, usage drops. Why? Because the novelty wears off, the pressure feels extrinsic, and people begin to game the system or quit entirely.

App B, on the other hand, does something different. It helps you set meaningful goals, gives you control over how you track progress, adjusts the challenge to match your fitness level, and offers subtle feedback after each session. There are no flashy rewards. But you feel yourself improving. You feel ownership. You come back not for points, but for progress.

App A uses surface gamification. It focuses on behavior. App B applies **Non-Skinnerian Gamification**. It focuses on motivation. One rewards movement. The other builds it into your identity.

Now imagine that same difference applied to your entire organization.

Sales Performance: Transactional vs Transformational

A software company rolls out a new sales contest. Every deal closed adds points. The top three sellers each month receive cash bonuses and public praise. Engagement rises briefly, but resentment starts to grow. The same people win every time. Collaboration drops. Knowledge hoarding increases. Junior reps disengage.

Meanwhile, a competitor takes a different approach. They build a sales experience where each rep can see their personal learning path, track skill growth, and get immediate feedback on key behaviors. Milestones are personalized. Reflection is built in. Mentorship is rewarded. The result is not just more sales but more learning, stronger culture, and higher retention.

Learning and Development: Points or Progress?

An organization launches a training portal where employees can earn badges and unlock levels by watching videos. After the first two weeks, engagement drops. People skip through content to collect rewards. They retain very little. The program looks successful on the dashboard, but fails in practice.

Another team builds learning journeys based on context, curiosity and autonomy. Each module starts with a problem to solve, not a quiz to pass. Feedback is instant. Progress is visible. Learners choose their path, collaborate with peers, and reflect on what they have applied. The experience is active, not passive.

One system rewards completion. The other gamifies learning.

Onboarding: Pressure or Participation?

A company uses leaderboards to speed up onboarding. New hires are ranked based on how quickly they finish their checklist. It creates urgency, but also anxiety. Some rush. Others feel overwhelmed. Many complete the tasks without truly understanding the why behind them.

In contrast, another company structures onboarding as a narrative journey. New hires unlock chapters as they explore core ideas, meet key people, and reflect on early experiences. They experience progress not just for finishing tasks, but for asking questions, sharing insights, and supporting others. The system guides, but does not control.

The first system triggers results through reward. The second system develops identity, mastery, and long-term excellence, leading to results.

One design pushes for compliance. The other invites contribution

THE MYTH SECTION

Now we begin to explore how what we call non-Skinnerian Gamification, if done right, becomes a core pillar of Intrinsic Performance Design.

Myth 1: Gamification Means Giving People Points, Badges, and Leaderboards

This is the most widespread belief about gamification. And on the surface, it makes sense. Most examples people see involve some form of points, badges, or leaderboards. They are easy to implement. They are visually clear. They promise motivation. For many companies, this is the beginning and the end of their gamification strategy.

But while these elements can create a short burst of activity, they also create something else. A trap.

What looks like motivation is often just momentum powered by novelty. And novelty fades quickly.

Points, badges, and leaderboards offer the appearance of progress. They give people something to chase and a reason to start. In the early days, usage spikes. People compare scores, they compete, and collect.

But then something happens.

Engagement drops. People lose interest. The excitement wears off. And what remains is not deeper motivation but a system that needs to be constantly refueled with more rewards, more incentives, and more pressure.

This is not a design flaw. This is the natural limit of extrinsic motivation.

Why Extrinsic Rewards Break Down

External rewards condition people to act for the sake of the reward. Over time, the activity itself becomes secondary. Once the reward is no longer appealing, the behavior disappears. What began as a motivational tool becomes a dependency.

Even worse, reward-heavy systems can backfire socially. Leaderboards often reward the top five percent while quietly demotivating everyone else. People at the top may feel proud, but those below often feel invisible or inadequate. You may like the people above you less, and the people below you may resent your position. It creates a culture of comparison, not connection.

And here is the irony. Most companies that install leaderboards are not trying to create internal competition. They want collaboration. They want knowledge sharing. They want teams that support each other. But the system they install sends the opposite message.

The message is subtle, but the impact is deep. Every piece of data you show is a framing device. Leaderboards frame work as a race. They show winners and losers. They create a zero-sum game, whether you intend it or not.

This does not mean extrinsic rewards have no place. But if they dominate the system, they will dominate the culture. And that culture may be completely misaligned with the values your company aims to stand for.

The belief that gamification is about points and prizes is not just misleading, it is a dangerous oversimplification. And it has led many organizations to misunderstand the true potential of motivational design.

Info Box: What Are Zero-Sum Activities, and Why Do They Matter?

A zero-sum activity is one where, for every winner, there must be a loser. Think of a pie: if I take a bigger slice, you get less. Most competitive games and classic leaderboards are built on this logic. My gain is your loss.

The trouble is, ze thinking seeps into culture. It turns colleagues into rivals, collaboration into competition, and progress into a frantic scramble for position. In business, this is a recipe for hoarding, backstabbing, and a chronic allergy to risk.

But here's the twist: most of modern work, and, dare I say, most of life, isn't zero-sum at all. Value can be created, not just divided. Teams can grow the pie, not just fight for crumbs. When you design systems that reward only the top of the leaderboard, you're not just picking winners, but you're manufacturing losers.

And that, as any behavioral economist will tell you, is a great way to drain motivation, stifle innovation, and breed mediocrity. The best organizations know: the real game is non-zero-sum. The goal isn't to beat each other. It's to win together.

Myth 2: If People Are Participating, They Must Be Engaged

At first glance, this belief feels hard to argue with. Participation looks like success. People are logging in, completing tasks, earning points, and checking boxes. Dashboards light up with activity. It feels like the system is working.

But activity is not the same as engagement. Just because someone is showing up does not mean they are invested. In fact, high participation can often mask low motivation.

This is one of the most common misinterpretations in gamified systems. The assumption is that if people are doing something, they must care about it. In reality, however, participation often has reasons that have nothing to do with real motivation.

The Illusion of Involvement

Extrinsic rewards can drive participation, but they often do so at the cost of depth. People complete actions to earn points, not because the action matters. Tasks become transactional. The system becomes a loop of earning and claiming, not exploring and understanding.

In educational settings, this can mean students rush through content for badges while missing the point of the material. In the workplace, employees may complete surface-level tasks to earn recognition while avoiding the work that requires deep focus or creative effort.

The result is a system full of movement but lacking momentum. People are active but not engaged. The structure may look busy, but it is hollow underneath.

The Shift Away from Purpose

When the system overemphasizes rewards, it can blur or even erase the original goal. People start optimizing for the reward, not the outcome. This creates what looks like progress but is actually drift.

Let's take the fitness app from the example before. If both, light and heavy workouts yield reasonable points, most users will choose the path of least resistance. The app is technically being used, but the deeper goal of building strength or resilience is quietly lost.

In learning environments, students may repeat easy tasks that yield quick wins instead of challenging themselves to stretch. They stay active, but they stop growing.

This is the danger of confusing participation with engagement. The system becomes a scoreboard, not a journey. People move within it, but not toward anything meaningful

The Trap of Quantification

Another problem lies in what most gamified systems choose to measure. Points and badges are easy to track, so they become the main currency. But they also reduce complex human behavior into simplified data.

This creates a bias toward what can be counted, even if it is not what matters most.

In schools, students focus on correct answers instead of critical thinking. In companies, employees chase metrics instead of solving problems. Quantification creates the illusion of clarity while quietly narrowing the definition of success.

Real engagement is messy. It involves struggle, insight, exploration, and emotion. These things are harder to measure, but they are also what make progress real.

The False Comfort of Activity

The most dangerous part of this myth is how reassuring it feels. Participation is visible, it is reportable, and it tells a comforting story. But it often hides the truth.

The truth is that shallow engagement rarely lasts. When the rewards stop, the behavior stops. When the system becomes predictable, people tune out. And when people participate without meaning, they learn to game the system rather than grow through it.

This is why so many gamification efforts plateau or collapse after the initial spike. They create performance theater without creating performance culture.

Participation is not engagement. It is just the first layer. And if the deeper layers are never designed, the system will always fall short of its promise.

Myth 3: The Fun in Gamification Comes from Reaching the Goal

Many organizations believe the magic of gamification lies in getting people to complete specific tasks. The thinking goes like this: define a goal, set a path, guide users through it, and reward them at the end. If people are reaching the finish line, the system must be working.

This belief feels safe. It gives structure. It creates measurable outcomes. It mimics traditional models of productivity. But what it actually creates is a fragile, one-dimensional experience. It removes the very ingredients that make real engagement possible.

Because the truth is, when interaction is built around rigid paths and fixed rewards, it may drive short-term compliance, but it kills long-term motivation.[18]

The Trap of Directed Play

Directed play is attractive to organizations because it guarantees completion. Directed play means that you decide what the user should do, when they should do it, and how they are rewarded for it. From a control perspective, this is ideal. It produces clean data. It standardizes progress, and it feels efficient.

But it also turns users into passengers. It limits their ability to explore, choose, or deviate. And once the path is completed, there is nothing left to do.

Directed play may look like engagement, but often it is just obedience in disguise.

The Loss of Autonomy

One of the first casualties of directed play is autonomy. When users follow predefined steps to earn rewards, their decisions no longer belong to them. They act to complete, not to discover. And once choice disappears, motivation fades.[19]

People stop asking what matters to them. They start asking what gets the most awareness from the system. The experience becomes passive. They follow instructions. They chase outcomes. But they stop thinking, caring, or growing.

In learning platforms, this shows up as students who complete assignments for points without absorbing the material. In professional settings, it appears as employees who finish training modules without applying what they learned. In both cases, the system measures movement, but not meaning.

The Roadblock to Mastery

Mastery thrives on challenge, curiosity, and self-direction. It depends on freedom to experiment and space to improve over time. Directed play restricts all of this. It funnels everyone through the same journey, with the same praise, toward the same finish line.

This creates uniformity, but not excellence.

When users cannot explore topics that matter to them, cannot set personal challenges, and cannot grow at their own pace, mastery becomes impossible. The result is shallow competence. Tasks get done, but growth is limited.

The Illusion of Progress

Structured paths make progress easy to track, but that kind of progress can be misleading. People move through the system, but often without engagement. They check the boxes. They earn the reward. Then, often, they leave.

In fitness apps, for example, users might choose the easiest workouts that still earn rewards. In loyalty programs, customers might chase quick wins that do not reflect true brand connection. In education, students might focus on getting through the lesson, not learning from it.

What appears as progress is often just completion without commitment.

The Danger of One-Size-Fits-All

Directed play creates homogenized experiences. Which might perhaps be the exact reason why organizations want it to work. Everyone is expected to move through the same steps in the same order. But people are not the same. They have different goals, different motivations, and different ways of learning or performing.

A single path cannot capture this diversity. And when systems ignore individuality, they alienate the very people they are trying to engage.

Some users will follow along. Others will quietly disengage. And the rest will disappear entirely.

Why the Finish Line is Not Enough

When gamification is treated as a way to get people to the finish line, it misses the point. Engagement does not come from finishing something. It comes from how people feel while they are doing it.

If the only satisfaction comes at the end, most people will not stay long enough to care.

This is why systems built around directed play struggle to create lasting engagement. They motivate briefly. Then they flatten. And eventually, they fail.

Because the fun in gamification does not come from reaching a goal. It comes from the freedom to pursue one.

Myth 4: You Can Just Add Gamification On Top of What Already Exists

This is a popular misconception in the field and probably the biggest pitfall. Many believe that gamification is a simple enhancement. Something you sprinkle on top of an existing system to make it more engaging. Add a few points. Throw in a badge. Maybe launch a leaderboard or add some playful avatars. The system stays the same, but now it has a game layer.

This is called the additive approach. And on paper, it looks appealing. It seems quick to implement. It avoids changing the core processes. It creates the impression of progress without requiring structural redesign.

But this is also why many gamification efforts fail repeatedly.

Because adding game elements on top of uninspiring systems does not transform them. It decorates them. It distracts from their flaws instead of addressing them.

The Superficial Fix That Creates Deeper Problems

The additive approach gives the illusion of engagement. For a brief period, users respond to the novelty. Activity increases. Participation spikes. Dashboards look promising.

But underneath, nothing has changed.

The work is still uninspiring. The process still lacks meaning. The system still fails to connect with how humans actually engage, learn, or perform. Game elements become cosmetic. They feel bolted on rather than built in.

And users notice. Quickly.

When game mechanics feel disconnected from the activity, they lose credibility. People stop seeing them as meaningful. They become noise. And when the novelty wears off, so does the participation.

A Misalignment That Undermines the Goal

The deeper issue is misalignment. If gamification, like any other behavioral design approach, is not integrated into the core of the experience, it begins to compete with the original purpose. They focus on the superficial layer instead of the real activity. The solution becomes a distraction.[20]

In corporate training, employees may click through modules to simply progress through the narratives. In customer loyalty programs, users might participate just enough to unlock discounts without ever forming a genuine connection to the brand.

The system becomes busy, but not effective.

Cosmetic Design Cannot Hide Friction

When a system is fundamentally unmotivating or disjointed, gamification will not fix it. It may even make it worse.

Imagine a broken onboarding process that simply adds a leaderboard. Or a disengaging course that now gives stars for every page clicked, and offers a separate narrative to cover up for boring content. Instead of solving the core problem, the gamified layer draws attention to it. It becomes a reminder that something is being covered up.

Users sense when the design is shallow. They feel it when rewards are not tied to real progress. And yes, they probably also appreciate the effort to offer a less boring alternative, with the added layer, but it makes it even more obvious how boring the real course is.

The False Comfort of Quick Wins

The additive approach survives because it offers quick wins. It requires less effort upfront. It avoids hard conversations about how the system itself needs to change. It allows teams to say, "We gamified it" without ever changing the foundation.

But these quick wins are short-lived. They create shallow engagement that fades fast. And they often delay the real work of building systems that actually support motivation and performance.

Cosmetic solutions feel easier. But they cost more in the long run.

When Gamification Is Treated Like a Skin, It Fails Like One

Gamification is not a feature. It is a design approach. It only works when it shapes how people interact, how progress feels, and how meaning is experienced inside the system itself.

If the system underneath is unengaging, no layer of points or prizes can make it work.

The belief that gamification can simply be attached to what already exists is not just misguided. It is one of the primary reasons gamification has underdelivered in many industries.

Until it is treated as a core experience, it will continue to fall short.

Myth 5: Games Are Fun Because We Compete Against Each Other

This belief runs deep. Many assume that the secret to gamification lies in igniting competitive fire. Add a leaderboard. Rank people. Offer prizes to the top performers. Let the thrill of winning drive the energy.

For a while, it seems to work, as engagement spikes, the top players push harder and the metrics look strong. But a different picture begins to emerge, as soon as you dare take a closer look.

Only a small group is thriving. Others are quietly withdrawing.

The Narrow Appeal of Competition

Leaderboards are easy to build and easy to explain, because they make performance visible and they appeal to those who already enjoy competition. In sales departments or academic environments where status and ranking are familiar, this can generate momentum.

But competition is not a universal motivator. It energizes some and alienates many. Most people do not perform best when they feel compared, ranked, and outpaced. They perform best when they feel supported, challenged, and connected.

When a system is built on the logic of winners and losers, it creates a culture that only rewards a fraction of the people inside it.

The Win-Lose Trap

Competitive mechanics reinforce a zero-sum mindset. Someone's success implies someone else's failure. That framing changes how people behave. It shifts focus from personal growth to social comparison. It encourages shortcuts, gaming the system, and even sabotage.

In learning environments, students stop helping each other. In workplaces, teams start protecting their turf. Collaboration fades. Knowledge is withheld. Trust erodes.

What began as an attempt to motivate can end up creating division.

The Quiet Cost of Ranking Low

Leaderboards do not just reward the top. They broadcast who is at the bottom. For those who struggle to climb the ranks, the system becomes a source of shame. The result is not motivation. It is withdrawal.

Many people do not fill out feedback forms, opt into challenges, or raise their hand to contribute. They do not withhold participation because they are lazy or uncommitted, but because the system has already told them they are not good enough.

These users are not underperforming. They are under-engaged by design.

The Misleading Metrics of Competition

Competitive systems often rely on simple metrics that are easy to measure like points, completions and counts, but do not always reflect what matters.

You can win a game by repeating low-effort tasks. You can climb a leaderboard by checking boxes. None of this means the person is learning, growing, or improving.

When competition becomes the goal, people optimize for the scoreboard, not for the outcome. And once that scoreboard is no longer interesting, they stop playing.

Not Everyone Wants to Beat Others

There is a fundamental truth often ignored in gamified design: many people are not playing to win, but they are playing to belong.[21]

They want to contribute. They want to improve. They want to feel progress in a meaningful way. These motivations are powerful, but they do not thrive in a classic win-lose environment. They thrive in systems built for inclusion, collaboration, and shared success, what is called a non-zero-sum activity.

The belief that games are fun because they are competitive confuses one type of motivation with the diverse reasons people play.

Yes, humans like to win. But most often, we love the process of growth that precedes the final win. Most people enjoy getting better. Most people stay engaged when they feel connected to others and to something that matters.

Competition is not wrong. But when it dominates the system, it pushes out other drivers of motivation that are often more sustainable, more human, and more effective.

Myth 6: People Want Everything to Be Easy, Quick, and Rewarding

This belief has quietly shaped the way many gamified systems are designed. The assumption is simple: if you want people to engage, make things as easy as possible. Keep the steps short. Make the tasks light. Give rewards early and often. Everyone wins.

At first glance, this approach seems logical. We live in a fast-paced world. Attention is short. People are busy. So why not remove friction, simplify tasks, and deliver instant gratification?

Because that's not what really drives us.

The deeper truth is that people don't value what costs them nothing. They don't remember what didn't challenge them. And they don't stay engaged with systems that expect nothing from them.

Do not confuse obtaining the desired behavior once with really motivating someone.

The Shallow Appeal of Immediate Wins

Yes, there is short-term satisfaction in easy tasks and quick rewards. Checking off a to-do list. Earning a badge after five minutes. Seeing points add up.

But what feels good for a moment rarely holds meaning over time. The brain may respond to the dopamine spike, but it doesn't attach significance to it. Once the novelty fades, so does the engagement.

This is how many gamified systems end up full of activity but without effective bonding.

Look at where people voluntarily spend their time: in complex games, challenging sports, intricate hobbies, and creative pursuits. These activities are not easy. They are not quick. And their rewards are often subtle or delayed.

People spend weekends learning strategy games with steep learning curves. They train for marathons. They teach themselves instruments. They take on difficult projects not because they want fast success, but because they want the satisfaction that comes from earning it.

They also do it together. Choirs rehearse the same passage until the harmony locks. Climbing partners take turns belaying and help each other through the crux. Kitchen brigades perfect timing until a service flows. Neighbors turn a vacant lot into a garden. The reward is not only skill. It is trust, belonging, and the quiet pride of shared craft.

If ease were the ultimate motivator, none of these things would exist.

The Joy Is in the Struggle

Real motivation comes from progress that costs something. From challenges that stretch us. From the feeling of moving forward through difficulty.

We do not bond with systems that hand us success. We bond with systems that respect us enough to demand something.

Games are not designed to get easier over time. They get harder. And that is exactly why people keep playing.

No game designer adds levels that take less effort just to give out more points. The design logic is the opposite: *the more you grow, the more we'll challenge you*. It is even a promise.

This reflects something deeply human. We want to rise. We want to overcome it. We want to feel the moment when effort turns into mastery.

The Mistake of Over-Simplifying Experience

In gamified systems, oversimplification often creates a checkbox mentality. People do the minimum required to collect the reward. They race to the finish line, not because the journey was engaging, but because they want it to be over.

This is not engagement. It is avoidance with a nice interface.

The myth of easy, quick, and rewarding sounds efficient. But it produces systems that are hollow. They do not ask much from users, and in return, they do not give much either.

The Challenge of Modern Performance

In today's world, where value comes from creative thinking, deep learning, and complex problem-solving, the easy path is rarely the right one.

If gamification is going to support real performance, be it cognitive, emotional, or social, it cannot avoid challenge. It must learn to work with it.

Because people don't stay where things are easiest. They stay where they grow.

Myth 7: Gamification Makes Everything Fun

Many people assume that gamification turns every task into a game. People assume that once you add game elements, any activity, no matter how dull, tedious, or difficult, becomes instantly fun. Suddenly, expense reports feel like Candy Crush. Compliance training feels like Mario Kart.

This belief is comforting. It suggests we can make anything enjoyable with the right mechanics. But it is also misleading. Because gamification is not about entertainment. It is about involvement. And those two things are not the same.

The Misunderstanding of the "Fun Switch"

Many see gamification as a fun switch. Add points, levels, or badges, and boring tasks become exciting. But that assumes that all people need is distraction or sugar-coating to enjoy their work.

That is not how motivation works.

Fun, especially the kind we associate with games, comes from freedom, challenge, surprise, and voluntary effort. In most real-world situations where gamification is applied, like education, healthcare, or the workplace, those conditions are limited by necessity. There, people are not playing along because they want to. They are participating because they have to.

This changes everything.

The Role of Voluntariness

Philosopher Bernard Suits once defined a game as a voluntary attempt to overcome unnecessary obstacles. That word 'voluntary' is critical. The joy of games depends on the fact that we choose to play. We accept the rules because we want the challenge. We keep playing because we enjoy the process.

"A game is the voluntary attempt to overcome unnecessary obstacles"

SUITS, BERNARD. (1978). THE GRASSHOPPER: GAMES, LIFE AND UTOPIA. UNIVERSITY OF TORONTO PRESS.

In contrast, most tasks in organizations are not chosen. They are assigned. People do them because they are required, not because they are intrinsically drawn to them. This does not make gamification useless. It makes its goal different.

The job of gamification is not to recreate the pure fun of games. Its job is to design necessary tasks in a way so that humans can find joy in doing them.

Gamification Enhances, It Does Not Replace

A good gamified system does not replace your favorite game. It does not pretend that payroll processing or safety training is suddenly a source of joy. What it can do is make those tasks more satisfying by increasing autonomy, improving feedback, creating progress loops, and introducing small elements of surprise.

This moves the task closer to the enjoyable end of the spectrum. Not all the way, but far enough to matter.

Gamification is not magic. It is context design that does not change the nature of the task but it changes the way people experience it.

The Danger of Overpromising

When organizations believe gamification will make everything fun, they design with the wrong goal in mind. They chase trends. They build for entertainment. And when people are not laughing or cheering, they assume the system has failed.

But involvement does not require laughter. It requires meaning. It requires a challenge. It requires a sense of progress and ownership.

Fun can be part of the experience, but it is not the benchmark of success. The real measure is whether people feel more connected to the task. Whether they care more, learn more, or improve faster.

Why This Myth Must Die

The myth of universal fun sets gamification up to fail. It creates unrealistic expectations. It invites shallow design. And most importantly, it distracts from what actually matters.

People do not need their tasks to be turned into video games. They need those tasks to feel more human. They need systems that acknowledge their effort, respect their autonomy, and reward their progress with a path to mastery, and not just with points.

Gamification is not about making everything fun. It is about making important things more engaging, especially when they are not fun to begin with.

That is where its real power lies.

Myth 8: Intrinsic Motivation Is Always the Goal

This one sounds so right that most people never question it. The idea that we should all aim to be intrinsically motivated to do work because we love it, not because we're told to, is appealing. It feels enlightened. It promises a world where joy meets productivity and passion powers performance.

But when you stop and actually examine it, this belief begins to fall apart.

The truth is not that intrinsic motivation is weak. It is powerful. The problem is that it is not always possible, appropriate, or even desirable.

The Limits of Passion-Driven Design

Picture a warehouse. Workers are moving packages from one place to another. The task is repetitive, time-bound, and essential. Is it realistic - or even fair - to expect that intrinsic motivation will drive these behaviors?

Trying to turn these tasks into a source of flow or personal meaning does not make the actual activity better. On the contrary, it makes the motivational design feel disconnected from reality. People are smart. They recognize when a system is pretending that a grind is actually a joy. And that undermines trust.

There are countless examples like this. Compliance checklists in healthcare. Data entry in logistics. Safety drills in aviation. These tasks are not designed for creativity. They are designed for consistency. In these cases, clear instructions and reliable rewards often outperform any attempt to spark inner passion.[22]

The Spectrum of Motivation

According to Self-Determination Theory[23] motivation comes in six distinct types. From *amotivation* at the lowest level to *intrinsic motivation* at the highest. Between these two poles lies a wide spectrum: *external regulation*, *introjected* motivation, *identified* motivation, and *integrated* motivation.[24]

Each has its place. Each is useful in the right situation

Info Box: The Six Motivation Types[25]

1. Amotivation

This is the state where someone has no motivation to act. They do not see the point of the task and often feel disconnected or helpless. It is not the same as laziness. It usually comes from confusion, burnout, or not understanding why something matters.

2. External Regulation

This is motivation driven by rewards or punishments. People do the task because they want to get something or avoid consequences. It works well for simple or repetitive tasks where clarity and efficiency are important.

3. Introjected Regulation

Here, people act because of internal pressure. They want to avoid guilt, shame, or a feeling of failure. This often looks like motivation from the outside but can lead to stress or long-term disengagement because it is rooted in self-criticism.

4. Identified Regulation

This is when someone sees value in the task. Even if the task itself is not enjoyable, they believe it is important. A person might not love filling out reports, but they do it because they understand how it helps the team or supports a goal they care about.

5. Integrated Regulation

At this level, the behavior is part of the person's identity. They do it because it reflects who they are and what they stand for. A mentor who spends time developing young colleagues might do so not for a reward but because it fits their sense of self.

6. Intrinsic Motivation

This is when someone does something simply because they enjoy it. It feels interesting or satisfying. The activity itself is the reward. People are often most creative and focused when acting from this type of motivation. However, this type is also highly sensitive to external pressure or poor design.

Pretending that intrinsic motivation is the only valid form is like saying that the only good tool is a hammer. It ignores the complexity of behavior and the diversity of environments we work in.

Sometimes, the job-to-be-done simply needs to be done. And the best way to get it done is with clarity, structure, and external reinforcement.

This knowledge about the six types of motivation is not a theoretical detour. It is a central foundation for everything that follows in the rest of this book. Many of the tools, decision models, and strategic approaches we will introduce in Part 3 are built on exactly this understanding. If at any point you feel unsure about which kind of motivation fits a particular context or why a certain intervention is not working, this is the section to come back to. These motivation types will help you make smarter decisions and design with greater clarity and nuance. Keeping this framework in mind will make your use of the Drive Method significantly more effective.

When Intrinsic Motivation Backfires

In many organizations, well-meaning leaders try to inject passion where none belongs. They talk about purpose while pushing through tasks that require precision, not inspiration. They design gamification systems aimed at igniting joy in environments that actually need reliability.

This leads to a mismatch between the message and the method. It creates cognitive dissonance. And people notice.

Worse, it wastes design resources. It asks for emotional energy where only behavioral clarity is needed. It also devalues the genuine experience of intrinsic motivation by trying to apply it everywhere.

Strategic Motivation Design Is the Real Goal

The smarter move is to design with realism. The goal is not to turn every task into a passion project. The goal is to align the job-to-be-done with the most effective behavior, and therefore with the appropriate kind of motivation.

Sometimes, that means leaning into extrinsic tools like clear feedback, structured incentives, visible milestones. Other times, it means building systems that allow for autonomy, mastery, and relatedness. The key is knowing which to use when.

The **Behavioral Solution Matrix** in section three of this book answers exactly this questions and helps you map behavior against context, so you are not applying motivation blindly. It prevents wasted effort. It ensures that the system fits the job.

Intrinsic Is Not the Holy Grail

There is no moral hierarchy of motivation. Intrinsic is not pure. Extrinsic is not corrupt. They are both tools. You use the one that fits the task, the context, and the person.

What matters is not whether people are intrinsically or extrinsically motivated. What matters is whether they are effectively and appropriately motivated to do what needs to be done.

Designing for motivation does not mean romanticizing every job. It means treating human behavior with respect. It means selecting the right lever for the right task.

And sometimes, it means saying no to gamification altogether when it does not serve the system.

Myth 9: Motivation Is an Individual Problem

"Some people are just more motivated than others."

It's a phrase you'll hear in countless leadership meetings, performance reviews, and hallway conversations. The implication is clear: motivation is a fixed trait, like height or eye color. You either have it or you don't. And if someone isn't performing, well...maybe they're just not motivated enough.

This myth is comforting. It provides a convenient explanation when things go wrong. It shifts responsibility away from systems, culture, and leadership, and directly onto the shoulders of the individual.

But this is only half the truth.

The False Assumption of "Motivated People"

If motivation were purely individual, we'd expect high performers to thrive in any environment. But they don't. Even top talent can struggle in toxic cultures, confusing systems, demotivating workflows, or just another context. And conversely, average performers can become exceptional when the conditions are right.

Motivation doesn't only live inside people like an innate ability. It is also dependent on context.

Often, people are not underperforming because they lack inner drive. Often, they are underperforming because their environment blocks, distorts, or starves that drive.

The High Cost of This Myth

When leaders believe motivation is just an individual problem, they default to three damaging behaviors:

- **Blame**: "She's just not hungry enough."

- **Pressure**: "Let's raise the targets and see who steps up."

- **Replacement**: "Let's hire someone more driven."

All three are short-term, reactive, and costly.

Even worse, this mindset creates cultures of quiet shame. Employees learn to mask burnout. They avoid asking for help. They internalize systemic problems as personal failure. Over time, this erodes trust, safety, engagement, and the very motivation companies claim to be chasing.

What the Science Actually Says

Research from Self-Determination Theory, behavioral psychology, and workplace engagement shows again and again:[26]

Motivation is not a trait. It's a state. And that state is shaped by:

- Autonomy and choice

- Social belonging and psychological safety

- Clarity of purpose

- Feedback and progress

- The match between task type and motivational design

Why This Myth Must Be Broken

Treating motivation as an individual issue leads to short-sighted solutions and talent waste. But when you shift your lens and treat motivation as an outcome of design, everything changes.

You stop asking, "Why aren't people more motivated?"

And start asking, "What system are we putting them into?"

This reframing is a leadership unlock. It turns motivation from a mystery into a lever. And it lays the foundation for building environments where even average performers can achieve extraordinary results. Not because they changed, but because the system did.

Myth 10: Behavior Change Is About More Knowledge

"Once people know better, they'll do better."

It sounds logical. Reasonable. Even optimistic. And it underpins countless company initiatives—from compliance trainings to slide-deck rollouts to awareness campaigns that say "we just need to educate people."

But here's the problem: this idea confuses understanding with behavior.

It assumes people act like mini-rational economists. That once they have the right information, they will naturally make the right choices. As if human behavior were a spreadsheet, waiting to be updated.

And that's not how change works.

The Intention-Action Gap

If knowledge were enough, nobody would smoke. No one would procrastinate. Everyone would save for retirement and floss daily.

But we don't. Not because we lack information but because we lack alignment between what we know and what we feel, experience or find rewarding.

There's a massive chasm between intention and action. Between awareness and execution. Between knowing and doing. And this myth keeps companies trapped on the wrong side of it.

Why This Myth Persists in organizations

It's easy to believe that information drives behavior because information is easy to deliver.

Want people to act differently? Give them a workshop. A checklist. A webinar. It's scalable, cheap, and cognitively neat.

But it's also largely ineffective. Because behavior doesn't change when people *hear* a new idea. It changes when they *experience* a new reality.

That's why memo-based culture shifts almost always fail. That's why awareness campaigns produce tiny blips and then fade. That's why "best practices" sit in binders while actual behavior continues on autopilot.

The Power of Behavioral Design

This myth sets up the case for behavioral economics and design-led intervention.

It's not about adding more cognitive content. It's about changing the environment in subtle, powerful ways that shift behavior without requiring constant effort.

It's about:

- Creating friction for undesired behaviors and flow for desired ones

- Making good choices easier, faster, more visible, and socially reinforced

- Using commitment devices, feedback loops, and progress framing to trigger momentum

- Designing experiences that align how people act with how they want to feel

Behavioral change is not an information problem. It's a system design challenge.

Why This Myth Must Be Broken

As long as leaders believe knowledge drives action, they will keep investing in communication instead of construction. They will craft better PowerPoints while ignoring broken workflows. They will launch awareness campaigns when what's needed is behavioral scaffolding.

The organizations that thrive in the future won't be the ones that *teach* better. They'll be the ones that *design* better. They'll build systems that turn the right action into the easiest, most obvious next step. No memo required.

Because once people feel it, once they experience progress, once the system makes it real, that's when change happens. Not before.

Short Myth Recap

Before we build a better system, we need to be brutally honest about the broken assumptions that dominate today's engagement strategies. Here's what we've just exposed:

Myth 1: Gamification is about Points, Badges, and Leaderboards

The problem isn't the use of rewards. It's the overuse of rewards that don't connect to meaning, growth, or autonomy. What looks like motivation is often just a short-term sugar high.

Myth 2: Participation Equals Engagement

Just because someone shows up doesn't mean they care. Superficial activity is easy to generate. Deep engagement is not. We must stop confusing movement with meaning.

Myth 3: People Want Predefined Goals and Easy Paths

Directed play strips away autonomy. It creates uniformity instead of exploration. Engagement drops when users feel like passengers instead of players.

Myth 4: Gamification Is Something You Attach On Top

This additive approach results in decoration, not transformation. True engagement systems are built from the inside out, not layered on as cosmetic upgrades.

Myth 5: Games Are Fun Because We Compete

Competition motivates some, but excludes many. Most engagement comes not from beating others, but from belonging, progressing, and contributing to something larger.

Myth 6: People Always Want Things to Be Easy, Quick, and Rewarding

This assumption kills challenge, depth, and flow. People don't bond with what comes cheap. They bond with what demands something from them and helps them grow.

Myth 7: Gamification Makes Everything Fun

Gamification isn't here to turn boring tasks into entertainment. It is here to make necessary effort more engaging, more meaningful, and more human.

Myth 8: Intrinsic Motivation Is Always the Goal

Not every task needs passion. Some just need clarity and completion. Motivation should be designed strategically, not ideologically.

Myth 9: Motivation Is an Individual Problem

Motivation isn't a character trait. It's an environmental outcome. Treating it as personal failure excuses broken systems and leads to shame-based leadership.

Myth 10: Behavior Change Is About More Knowledge

If knowing was enough, change would be easy. Real behavior change happens through design, not education. People don't shift because they know but they shift because something feels different.

THE INSIGHT SECTION

What Science Knows but Industry Ignores

Now that we've dismantled the most persistent myths, the path forward becomes clearer...and more uncomfortable.

Because the real problem is not that we lack knowledge.

The science of motivation, engagement, and behavior has never been richer. Fields like neuroscience, evolutionary psychology, behavioral economics, and motivation theory have mapped out what actually drives human performance. We know how curiosity works. We understand the mechanics of flow. We have detailed models of what makes people care, persist, and grow.

The problem is that most organizations still operate as if none of this existed.

They continue designing systems based on outdated assumptions. They optimize for compliance instead of growth. They use pressure where purpose would work better. They bolt on gimmicks where structure is needed.

There's a growing gap between what science knows and what industries do.

That gap has a cost. It shows up in disengagement metrics, in wasted talent, in low-impact initiatives that look exciting on the surface but fail to create meaningful change underneath.

So before we explore how to design better systems, we need to pause.

We need to shine a light on the knowledge that is already out there, although ignored, overlooked, or misunderstood by organizations, and understand what it actually tells us about

human performance.
The science is clear. We just haven't applied it.

Let's examine what that science says, and why it matters now more than ever.

Insight #1: Progress Drives Persistence

"Almost There" Beats "Already Made It" Almost Every Time

Let's start with a little mischief.

If you wanted to design the perfect trap for the human brain, it wouldn't be a big prize. It wouldn't be guaranteed success. It would be the feeling of *almost winning*. That exquisite space between failure and triumph. Not because it gives us pleasure, but because it creates *possibility*.

This is what Harvard professor Teresa Amabile called *The Progress Principle*.[27] And what evolutionary psychology would call *completely bloody obvious*.

We are not wired to be satisfied. We are wired to keep going.

If rewards were enough, slot machines would be boring, cliffhangers would be annoying, and IKEA (see explanation box *The IKEA Effect*) would be out of business. But they're not. Because the genius of all these experiences lies not in *completion*, but in *incompletion*, and the delicious sense that the next effort might be the one that gets you over the edge.

Info Box: The IKEA Effect[28]

Let's be honest: if IKEA sold you a pre-assembled bookshelf, you'd probably treat it with the same reverence you reserve for a cardboard box after moving house: useful, but utterly forgettable.

Yet, hand you a flat pack, an Allen key, and a cryptic set of instructions, and suddenly you're Leonardo da Vinci with a hex wrench.

The result? You lavish disproportionate pride and affection on your wobbly creation, flaws and all. This is *The IKEA Effect*: our peculiar tendency to overvalue things we've had a hand in making.

It's a glorious quirk of human psychology. It is the proof that effort, even when it borders on mild suffering, is not only tolerated but cherished. In a world obsessed with efficiency and frictionless experiences, we forget that a little sweat equity isn't a bug; it's a feature. We love what we labor over, not despite the struggle, but because of it.

Progress is like a mirage. And motivation? That's what happens when you think you can finally reach it.

The Neuroscience of "Not Yet"

Here's the thing: we love progress. But only when we can *feel* it. Not in theory, but viscerally.

The final stretch of a marathon. The last chapter of a novel. The progress bar on a website creeping toward 100 percent. These things feel disproportionately motivating because they trigger what behavioral economists might call *psychological tailwind*. You don't just move forward, you're pulled forward.

This is why:

- People binge-watch a whole series once they hit episode 7

- Runners sprint the last 200 meters even when their lungs are on fire

- You clean your whole apartment just because you've done one room and now you're "on a roll"

- The progress doesn't just measure your effort. It multiplies it.

Why Most Motivation Systems Fall Flat on Their Faces

Sadly, most organizations are still stuck in what we might call **Completion Fetishism**. They reward the finish line. The final KPI. The goal ticked off the to-do list.

But this approach leaves vast stretches of psychological no man's land, long periods where effort feels invisible, progress feels uncertain, and motivation quietly vanishes like a polite dinner guest.

Even worse? Classic motivation systems, as well as classic gamification approaches, tend to amplify this mistake. They obsess over end states, badges, points, ranks. But what actually fuels effort is *feeling like you're just about to get something*, not having gotten it already.

The irony is thick: in trying to make people succeed, we've forgotten how people *want* to succeed: *incrementally*, *imperfectly*, *almost*.

Games Understand What MBAs Forgot

Video games are the behavioral design labs the corporate world still hasn't learned from.

No game is designed to let you win easily. In fact, the best ones are engineered so you fail most of the time. Just close enough to feel possible, just far enough to keep you coming back. If you won every time, you'd be bored stiff in minutes. The magic isn't in victory; it's in the delicious tension between failure and the promise of success.

That's why "almost" is the real hook. It's why we try again, and why we push forward. Because the brain sees proximity to success as a signal to double down, not give up.

The dopamine system (which we'll get to in the next insight) is tuned for progress, not payoff. This is why the illusion of progress often works better than actual rewards.

Want someone to complete a profile? Show them it's already 70 percent complete. Want them to come back tomorrow? Show them what they have already invested.

This isn't trickery. It's tuning into the brain's own motivational mechanics.

How to Design for the Edge of Success

If you want a performance system to work, stop designing it around finishing and start designing it around feeling almost finished.

Design mechanics that:

- Show progress constantly and visually
- Frame failure as being "just one step away"
- Provide micro-achievements that keep the fire alive

Remember: people don't quit because they're lazy. They quit either because the goal feels too far away or because it is too easy and not worth their time. But if you can make every action feel like the one that might tip the scales, you'll keep them coming back. Not because they're told to, but because they *want* to.

Final Thought: Progress Is the Crack Cocaine of Motivation

Forget perfection. Forget finish lines. What people crave is *momentum*.

So if you're building systems to sustain engagement, design for the moment just before success. Not the moment after. Because once people succeed, they stop. But when they *almost* succeed?

They try again.

And again.

And again.

That's not weakness.

That's human nature.

Insight #2: Dopamine Isn't About Having. It's About Hunting.

Let us begin with a heresy.

The world, or at least every HR department and most gamification designers, has fundamentally misunderstood dopamine. They imagine it like confetti: tossed into your brain when you finish something. You did it! Here's your neurochemical gold star! Job complete. Well done, you.

This is, to put it politely, behavioral hogwash.

The truth is far more interesting. And more useful. Dopamine doesn't reward you for having achieved something. It rewards you for believing you're about to.[29]

Think of dopamine not as the champagne at the finish line, but as the rumour of a bottle hidden just around the next corner. It doesn't celebrate your success. It propels your pursuit.

This is not some eccentric theory whispered in the halls of Cambridge. It's backed by neuroscientists like Robert Sapolsky. When does the biggest dopamine spike happen? Not at the jackpot. But just before you think you're going to hit it.

We are not pleasure seekers. We are possibility seekers.

Info Box: Dopamine is About Anticipation And Pursuit, Not Just The Pleasure of Reward.

Most people think of dopamine as the "pleasure chemical": the thing your brain releases when you get something you want, like a piece of chocolate or a big win. But Sapolsky's research (and the broader field of neuroscience) turns this idea on its head. Dopamine isn't really about the pleasure of having; it's about the excitement of *almost* having.

In experiments with animals (and humans), dopamine spikes not when the reward arrives, but when there's a cue that a reward *might* be coming. For example, if a monkey sees a light that means food is on the way, its dopamine levels shoot up *before* the food arrives. If the food is guaranteed, the dopamine spike is smaller. But if there's uncertainty, like maybe the food comes, maybe it doesn't, the dopamine spike is even bigger. The brain loves the chase, the possibility, the "maybe."

What does this mean? It means we're wired to be motivated by the pursuit, not just the payoff. The thrill is in the hunt, the anticipation, the sense that success is just around the corner. That's why slot machines are so addictive, why cliffhangers keep us watching, and why "almost winning" is so compelling. The classic view of dopamine as a simple "reward chemical" misses the point: it's really the chemical of motivation, drive, and possibility.

In short: Dopamine is less about the joy of getting what you want, and more about the excitement of believing you *might* get it. That's what keeps us moving, striving, and coming back for more.

The Chase is the Cheese

A lab rat doesn't get addicted to cheese. It gets addicted to the possibility of cheese. This is why slot machines work, even though mathematically they're idiotic. It's why Tinder is addictive. And it's why you find yourself checking your email fifteen times a day hoping someone, somewhere, might send something that isn't a LinkedIn newsletter.

"In dopamine terms, maybe is more powerful than definitely. And soon is more motivating than now."

This is a problem if you're designing systems based on the now. Points, badges, rewards, those are all things. But motivation doesn't come from things. It comes from what might happen if...

Design for that and the entire game changes.

Why Most Gamification Is Like a Gift Shop That Only Sells Trophies

The traditional approach to gamification is to hand out rewards like candy on Halloween. Here's a badge. Here's a trophy. Here's a leaderboard to show off how brilliant Steve in Finance is, yet again.

But here's the thing: once the reward is handed out, it loses all its tension. It becomes inert. The magic is gone.

You wouldn't go to a cinema that starts with the ending. You wouldn't play a game where you win every time. Yet gamification systems often behave as if the solution to low motivation is simply to pump more certainty and more finality into the process.

But real motivation comes from ambiguity and proximity. The sense that you're nearly there. Almost. Just one more push.

Think of a progress bar at 91 percent. You want to finish. You can feel it pulling you forward. But if you make it too easy, say, give someone 100 points just for logging in, you get no movement. Only apathy.

Designing with Dopamine Means Designing for "Not Yet" (Insight #1)

So here's the big switch.

If you want to build motivational systems that work, stop designing for completion. Start designing for chase.

That means:

- Creating near-miss moments, not just win screens

- Offering glimpses of progress, not just confirmation of it

- Structuring experiences to feel like the next step is just out of reach

Think breadcrumb trail, not treasure chest.

People don't stick around because they've arrived. They stay because they have not yet fully arrived.

And If You Must Use Rewards… Be Devious About It

Now, if you're hell-bent on using classic rewards…fine. But here's a behavioral twist that almost no one uses. If you give people a reward before they do the task, they'll often work harder to deserve it.

Why? Because humans are, if nothing else, psychologically consistent. We hate cognitive dissonance. If I've already received something of value, my brain wants to believe I've earned it. So it backfills the effort.

The lesson? You don't need more carrots as a reward. You just need to use them as a resource for an upcoming task, and tell a better story about how they help.

Final Thought: Motivation Is Not a Finish Line. It's a Horizon.

The moment something is achieved, it loses power. The brain shifts. The pursuit fades. Motivation collapses. But if you can create a system where people always feel like they're about to break through, that is where the magic happens.

This is why Gamification may not be mainly about rewards. It's about movement.

Not the celebration, but the suspense.

And that, dear reader, is dopamine's real secret. It's not your victory drug. It's your voyage drug.

Insight #3: The Value of Meaningful Challenge

This is about the sweet seduction of struggle.

If you believe that engagement is created by removing effort, let me gently suggest you have confused *appeasement* with *enchantment*.

This is the great corporate delusion: that people want ease. That the path to motivation lies in reducing friction to zero. As if the highest form of satisfaction comes from doing absolutely nothing.

If that were true, the most addictive video game would be one where you simply press "Start" and watch the credits roll. No enemies. No obstacles. Just immediate victory and a confetti animation.

Spoiler alert: nobody would play that game.

And yet, this is exactly how most organizations design their so-called engagement strategies. They flatten everything. They remove difficulty. They smooth the path until it becomes a slide, only to discover that once people reach the bottom, they feel nothing.

Convenience is not the opposite of resistance. It is often the enemy of meaning.

Obstacles Aren't the Problem. They Are the Point.[30]

Let's revisit Bernard Suits' definition of games as "the voluntary attempt to overcome unnecessary obstacles."

Now think about that. Not just "obstacles" but *unnecessary* ones. Games are not about utility. They are about useless, joyful struggle.

This is what Raph Koster nails in *A Theory of Fun*. We do not enjoy games because they are relaxing. We enjoy them because they make us think. Because they *stretch* us. Because they reward *growth*, not ease.

Games are, quite literally, environments built to make people suffer voluntarily. And we pay for the privilege.

If that doesn't make you question the entire architecture of your incentive system, nothing will.

The Tragic Pursuit of "Low-Effort Engagement"

Most gamification fails for one simple reason: it tries to make work feel like a vending machine. Insert task. Get treat. Repeat.

In this model:

- Challenge is seen as friction.

- Effort is treated as a barrier.

- Complexity is viewed as the enemy.

And what you're left with is a shallow, hollow experience. Something that may drive compliance, but will never drive curiosity.

The result? Systems designed like children's sticker charts. Pretty, short-lived, and profoundly forgettable.

Why We Chase Mountains, Not Molehills

There is something oddly universal about the desire for challenge. People climb Mount Everest not because it's easy, but because it isn't. People spend weekends solving crosswords and assembling IKEA furniture not in spite of the effort, but *because of it.*

We love challenges that ask something of us, so long as they ask the *right* thing. The challenge must be difficult enough to matter, but not so impossible that it crushes us. This is what Mihaly Csikszentmihalyi called **Flow**: that magical zone where difficulty and ability dance together.

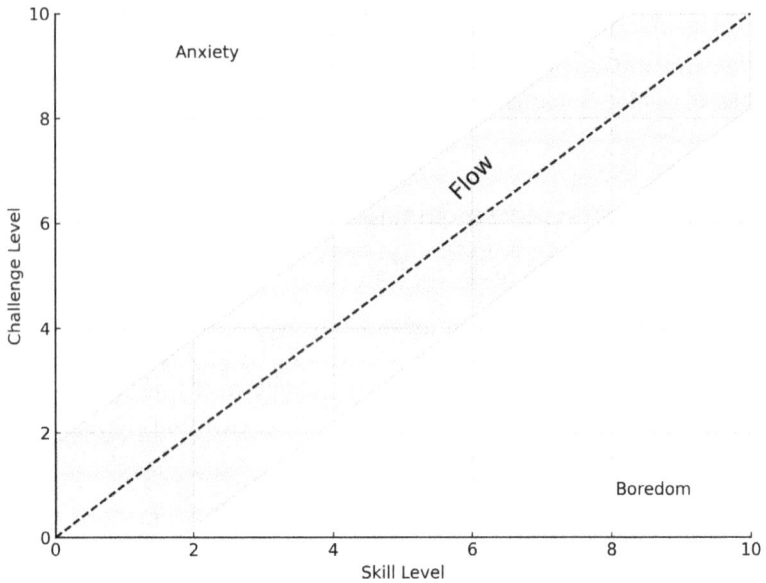

Figure 1: Flow channel. Author's illustration adapted from Mihaly Csikszentmihalyi, *Flow: The Psychology of Optimal Experience*, 1990.

Flow is not found in ease. It is found in edge.

This is why:

- Great games become more difficult as you play.
- Great sports create progressive mastery.
- Great teachers stretch you just far enough that the answer is within reach, but not within comfort.

And yet, most systems refuse to 'play this game'. They hand out rewards for breathing. They celebrate participation rather than progress. They fear challenge, when they should be *designing* for it.

A System That Respects You Enough to Challenge You

Here's a dangerous idea: challenge isn't the enemy of engagement. It is the signal that the activity *respects you*.

When something asks more of you, it is suggesting that you are capable of more. And when you meet that challenge, even partially, you don't just feel proud. You feel *hooked*.

You don't need prizes to do it again. The struggle was the reward.

This is the golden rule of the non-Skinnerian Gamification school of thought: We do not seek to entertain people. We seek to *respect* them.

We assume they are capable of more. We assume they want to grow. We assume that engagement is not about coddling, but about climbing.

Closing Thought: Why Meaning Requires Resistance

A world without obstacles is not a utopia. It is a flatland.

Ease may be efficient. But challenge creates *stories*. And meaning, as every great storyteller knows, is just difficulty remembered with affection.

So stop trying to make everything easy.

Design things that are *worth doing*.

Make systems that challenge people respectfully.

Because when people feel like they're getting better, they keep coming back. Not because of what they get at the end, but because of who they become along the way.

And that, my friends, is the real game we all want to play.

Insight #4: Paying People to Be Creative Is Like Paying a Plant to Grow Faster[31]

One of the great, silent tragedies of modern business is that it still thinks like a factory, even when there's nothing left to manufacture.

We see this everywhere. Bonuses for "ideation." Incentives for "innovation." Targets for "thinking outside the box." The results, as you might imagine, are dreadful. Not because people aren't creative, but because the *system* isn't.

It's like trying to grow a forest by shouting at the trees. Or watering them with Red Bull.

Most companies are still treating modern cognitive work like assembly line labor. And in doing so, they are not just missing the point, they are actively dismantling the very conditions required for people to think well.

A Tale of Two Tasks: Why Your KPIs Kill Innovation

Imagine two scenarios.

In the first, someone is asked to screw the same bolt into a machine 500 times a day. The goal is speed and precision. Mistakes cost money. Disruption is bad. Consistency is king.

In the second, someone is asked to figure out how to reduce customer churn in a global SaaS business. The answer isn't obvious. The solution isn't pre-defined. You need experimentation, mental simulation, wild ideas, unexpected metaphors.

Now, ask yourself: should both tasks be managed by the same performance system?

Of course not. One is repetition. The other is reinvention.

And yet, in far too many businesses, both are treated to the same motivational toolkit: bonuses, metrics, performance reviews, rankings. It's the psychological equivalent of prescribing the same drug for a headache and a heart transplant.

Extrinsic Motivation Works. Right Up Until the Moment It Doesn't.

Here's the uncomfortable truth: the carrot and stick approach works extremely well in situations where repetitive work is the dominant factor.

But in other situations? Especially when it comes to solving complex problems, they're not really helpful. They're almost harmful.

This has already been proven decades ago[32]. Researchers found that when you pay people to do a creative task, their performance *drops*. Give someone money to solve a puzzle, and their brain becomes less curious, less agile, less inventive. What was once playful becomes pressured. What was once open-ended becomes boxed in.

This is called **The Overjustification Effect**. Once you introduce a reward, people stop asking "What could I do?" and start asking "What do I need to do to get the reward?"[33]

Creativity vanishes. Compliance surges. Which would be lovely, if compliance ever invented anything.

The Irony of Incentivizing Innovation

If you try to motivate creativity using extrinsic levers, you'll end up with mimicry, not magic.

Think of a brainstorming session where people only speak up if their comment earns them visible brownie points. Think of a performance review that rewards "strategic risk-taking" but punishes every failed experiment. Think of a startup culture obsessed with metrics but terrified of ambiguity.

Incentivizing creativity is like putting a speedometer on a poem. It might give you numbers. It won't give you beauty.

Repetition Craves Rules. Creativity Craves Freedom.

This is the fundamental divide. Repetitive work thrives on predictability, clarity, and reward. Creative work thrives on ambiguity, autonomy, and play.

So when you design a motivation system, the first question is not "How do we motivate people?" but rather "What type of work are we trying to motivate?"

If it's repetitive, then yes, extrinsic incentives are efficient. They compress variability. They tighten compliance. They work well on the factory floor.

But if the work is creative? Then those same tools are about as useful as a chainsaw in a surgery.

What We Should Be Asking Instead

Modern work is a blend of the predictable and the exploratory. Which is why our motivational systems should also be blended. And adaptive.

We should stop asking "How do we get people to try harder?" and start asking "What kind of mindset does this work require?" Do we need precision or play? Obedience or imagination?

This is exactly why we built the Behavioral Solution Matrix, which you'll find in the next section. Because designing for performance isn't about choosing one motivation style. It's about choosing the right one, in the right context, for the right behavior.

You wouldn't use a light switch to control a drone show. So why use the same incentive structure to reward box-ticking AND breakthrough thinking?

Final Word: The Factory Is Dead. Stop Motivating Like It Isn't.

The tragedy is not that companies are bad at motivation. The tragedy is that they are brilliant at the wrong kind of motivation, applied to the wrong kind of work.

You don't get better jazz by raising the tempo of the metronome. You don't get more Picasso by measuring brushstrokes per hour.

Creative work needs different fuel.

So maybe it's time we stop pouring diesel into Teslas.

Insight #5: We Love the Bookshelf We Built Backwards[34]

Let's remember the example of IKEA. You spend three hours navigating a set of pictograms clearly designed by someone who hates humanity. You use a wrench that resembles a piece of orthodontic equipment. At some point, you attach the side panel upside down and are forced to take it all apart again.

But eventually, miraculously, it stands.

And what do you feel?

Pride. Deep, irrational, chest-thumping pride. Not because it's perfect. Quite the opposite. You know damn well you could have bought a pre-built shelf for less money and saved the three hours of existential self-loathing. But this one? This one is *yours*.

Studies show that when people build or shape something themselves, they irrationally overvalue it, even when it's objectively worse than alternatives.

Now here's the part most businesses fail to grasp:

The IKEA Effect doesn't just apply to furniture. It applies to **motivation**.

People don't engage more because the system is better. They engage more because they helped shape it.

The Fatal Flaw of Linear Motivation Systems

Look around at how most engagement systems are designed: workplace onboarding, corporate learning, self-improvement platforms.

They treat motivation like it's a conveyor belt. Step one, step two, earn your badge, collect your certificate, receive your dopamine. All very neat. All very efficient. All very... deadening.

Why? Because when people are placed on a path they didn't help create, they feel like passengers. Worse, they feel like luggage. And it turns out, very few people are motivated by being told where to sit and when to move.

Contrast this with games, side hustles, hobbies, or even assembling IKEA furniture. What makes these engaging isn't that they're smooth. It's that they're *yours*. You chose them. You shaped them. You messed them up and made them better.

It's the same reason why a lot of people love open-world video games. Not because they're told what to do, but because the story unfolds as they make decisions. It's *their* journey. Not a pre-written script.

The Magic of Emergent Progress

The idea that motivation needs to be delivered from above, via incentives, rules, or paths, is a relic of managerial overconfidence.

Here's the reality: People aren't inspired by being dragged toward a finish line. They are inspired by watching progress *unfold* based on their own choices.

This is the psychological gold that most gamified systems pave over. They mistake clarity for control. They believe people will be more engaged if everything is laid out clearly from the start. But in doing so, they rob the user of the single most powerful motivational force: the sense that this is *my* journey.

The future of performance systems isn't top-down. It's co-authored.

Design for Discovery, Not Delivery

The goal should not be to walk people through a story. It should be to let people co-*write* one.

That's why the **IntrinsicQ Performance Journey** (which is also introduced in Part 3) is built around progressive unfolding. Each step invites a decision. Each decision triggers a new step. The system becomes something you participate in, not something that happens to you.

In other words, it's not a linear path. It's a living path.

And yes, it's more complex to build. But that complexity is what makes it engaging. If people aren't writing their own story, they're just reading someone else's, and let's be honest, most corporate stories aren't exactly page-turners.

The Bottom Line: Never Rob People of Their Plot Twist

If you want someone to feel ownership, don't hand them a map and a destination. Give them a compass and a landscape. Let them get a bit lost. Let them struggle and decide and discover.

Because here's what we've learned:

Even when the task is harder. Even when the process is slower. Even when the outcome is messier.

If it feels like *mine*, I'll care more. I'll try harder. I'll stay longer. And I'll be proud. Even if one of the shelves is still upside down.

That is the real secret to engagement: Ownership.

Just give people a journey they get to shape, and they'll walk it. Happily. Even barefoot.

It is crucial to distinguish the value of challenge from the value of ownership. Meaningful challenge, as explored in Insight #3, is about the inherent joy and growth found in the struggle itself. The IKEA Effect, discussed in this Insight #5, is about the pride and connection we feel toward the result of that struggle. One makes the journey rewarding; the other makes the destination feel uniquely our own.

Insight #6: Systems Shape Signals

Let me begin with a paradox that would make any behavioral economist chuckle:
You can say all the right things, and still demotivate your team entirely.
Not because your message was wrong. But because the system around it whispered something else.

This is the overlooked engine room of organizational psychology: **systems are never neutral.** They're always sending signals. Constantly. Relentlessly. Whether you mean them to or not.

Take KPIs. You say your company values long-term thinking. Strategic depth. Collaboration. Yet every performance dashboard your employees see is structured around short-term numbers, individual output, and quarterly targets. You just told them "quality matters," but the dashboard says "speed is king."

Which one do you think they'll listen to?

"Design Has a Voice. Even When You're Silent."

Here's the trick: humans don't respond to abstract mission statements. They respond to *cues*. Psychological signals. Tiny nudges from their environment that tell them what *really* matters. And these cues come less from what leaders say and more from what systems imply.

You don't motivate a team by holding a speech about trust and empowerment.
You motivate them by stopping the requirement to cc five layers of hierarchy on every email.

You don't drive innovation by saying, "We value experimentation." You drive it by creating processes that *don't punish* failure with three weeks of paperwork.

You don't reinforce team spirit with a poster that says "We win together."
You do it by designing dashboards that show collective progress instead of individual league tables.

Most leaders completely underestimate this silent influence. They try to fix culture with words, while leaving their systems to scream the exact opposite.

Why Most Systems Are Sending the Wrong Message

Let's go back to dashboards for a second. We love them because they give an illusion of control. Color-coded, number-driven clarity. But every data presentation is a form of storytelling. And like any story, it comes with a frame.

Leaderboards frame performance as zero-sum.
Time-tracking software frames trust as optional.
Monthly sales rankings frame colleagues as competitors.
Micromanagement tools frame autonomy as a risk.

These frames are powerful. More powerful than any value statement or town hall announcement. Because they're not just information but interpretations baked into design.

In behavioral economics, this is called **choice architecture**. The way you structure options, feedback, and visibility shapes how people behave. Not because they're told to, but because they're nudged.

And here's the kicker: most companies are nudging people in the exact opposite direction of their declared values.

What This Really Means for Leaders

It means that if you want to change behavior, you have to audit more than processes.

You need to audit signals.

Ask yourself:

- What do our KPIs make people optimize for?

- What does our org chart make people believe about hierarchy and control?

- What do our meeting rituals imply about who gets to contribute?

- What behaviors are we subtly rewarding, even if we don't mean to?

This is a moment where motivation systems can go wrong. Not because they're badly intentioned. But because they're misaligned. They say one thing and structure another. And the brain, being the clever predictive engine it is, always follows structure.

The System Is the Message

When we talk about building motivational environments, what we're really saying is: *design systems that send the right signals*. Not just loud signals. Not just values-on-the-wall signals. But signals that *feel real* in the everyday trenches of work.

Because at the end of the day, performance doesn't emerge from what people hear. It emerges from what their environment tells them is safe, valuable, and possible.

Design your systems to whisper the right messages, and suddenly, motivation stops being a management problem. It becomes a cultural reflex.

Insight #7: Coherence Is the New Competitive Advantage

Let's talk about why the smartest people quietly quit when nothing adds up.

Let's begin with a little riddle:
What do high-potential employees, expensive consultants, and passionate changemakers all have in common?
They don't leave bad jobs. They leave incoherent systems.

You've seen it. The company with the beanbags and barista bar. The "future of work" mural painted on the wall. The strategic offsites about trust and innovation. And yet, somehow no one sticks around.

Why?
Because the words say one thing, the incentives say another, and the daily experience whispers something else entirely.

This isn't about hypocrisy. It's about **incoherence**.
A subtle, creeping dissonance between what people are told and what they actually live. And make no mistake: coherence

isn't a nice-to-have. It's now your most urgent source of competitive advantage.[35]

The Human Brain Is a Bullsh*t Detector

We like to think people disengage because they're lazy, distracted, or entitled. But often, they're just exhausted from playing a game whose rules don't make sense.

- Your onboarding says "we care about wellbeing."
  But your meeting culture burns out introverts and parents.

- Your values say "we believe in bold ideas."
  But your budgeting process penalizes risk and rewards predictability.

- Your mission says "people first."
  But your CRM tool is designed for surveillance, not trust.

These contradictions don't just annoy people. They **confuse** them. And the human brain hates confusion. Especially when it smells like betrayal.

This is where cynicism breeds. Not from bad intentions, but from mental friction. People are trying to connect belief to behavior, and the wires keep getting crossed.

Culture Isn't What You Say. It's What You Reinforce.

Coherence means that your systems, rituals, rewards, and signals all say the same thing.
It's what makes a place feel real. Predictable. Trustworthy.

Because coherence isn't about perfection. It's about alignment. People can handle pressure. They can handle change. What they can't handle is being told they're autonomous while being micromanaged. Or being told they're innovators while being given no room to explore.

Incoherence is a tax. On attention. On energy. On loyalty. And companies are paying it every single day. Whether they know it or not.

How Coherence Becomes a Strategic Weapon

Here's the magic: when coherence is high, people stop second-guessing everything. They stop scanning for subtext in every decision. They stop hedging, covering, gaming the system.

Instead, they start engaging.

Because now, finally, the game makes sense.

- The behaviors that are rewarded match the values on the wall.

- The systems that track performance match the work that actually matters.

- The feeling of being here...matches the story being sold out there.

Suddenly, performance stops being a tug-of-war between people and process. It becomes a flow. And that flow is what every culture designer is secretly trying to build, but few ever do.

Short Insight Recap

Insight 1: Progress Drives Persistence

People don't crave completion. They crave the feeling of being on the edge of a breakthrough. "Almost there" is more powerful than "already done." Motivation is not sustained by outcomes, but by the illusion of proximity. Great systems don't just track progress, they engineer it. Visibly, constantly, and emotionally.

Insight 2: Dopamine Isn't About Having. It's About Hunting.

We misunderstood dopamine. It's not released when we get the prize, but when we believe it's just around the corner. Motivation doesn't come from reward. It comes from pursuit. Effective systems don't deliver satisfaction, they spark curiosity and fuel the chase. The brain doesn't care that you've arrived. It wants to keep moving.

Insight 3: Making Things Easy Makes Them Pointless

Ease is not engagement. Challenge is. We don't fall in love with what's frictionless. We fall in love with what demands effort, teaches us something, and makes us better. Motivation isn't about removing obstacles. It's about designing the right ones. Ones that stretch, not crush.

Insight 4: Paying People to Be Creative Is Like Paying a Plant to Grow Faster

Extrinsic rewards work beautifully for repetitive tasks. But they kill creativity. They shift focus from exploration to compliance. Repetition thrives on clarity. Creation thrives on ambiguity, autonomy, and trust. One-size-fits-all motivation systems don't just underperform, they actively sabotage the performance they seek.

Insight 5: We Love the Bookshelf We Built Backwards

Ownership beats optimization. People value what they help create, even when it's messier or slower. Linear systems make people feel like passengers. But when a journey unfolds based on their decisions, motivation explodes. Engagement isn't about the path being smooth. It's about the path feeling personal.

Insight 6: Systems Shape Signals

It's not what leaders say. It's what systems imply. Dashboards, KPIs, workflows, all of them whisper values louder than any vision statement. Motivation dies in the gap between what's said and what's signaled. To change behavior, don't fix the message. Fix the architecture that delivers it.

Insight 7: Coherence Is the New Competitive Advantage

People don't burn out because of pressure. They burn out because nothing adds up. When values, behaviors, and systems contradict each other, trust erodes and performance crashes. Coherence between what you promise and what you design is no longer a luxury. It's a strategic necessity.

Connecting the Dots: From Dopamine to Design

The insights you've just explored are not isolated phenomena. They are deeply connected, forming a coherent and powerful model of how motivation truly functions. Think of it as a journey from the microscopic level of neurochemistry to the macro level of human experience. By connecting these dots, we can move from simply knowing interesting facts to understanding a complete system.

Here is how the pieces fit together:

It all begins with **dopamine**. As we've seen, dopamine is not a simple "pleasure chemical"; it is the neurochemical engine of pursuit. It is released not when we achieve a goal, but when we anticipate that we are getting closer. This biological mechanism is the foundational driver, the "hunting" instinct that pulls us forward.

This dopamine-driven pursuit is the "why" behind *The Progress Principle*. The feeling of being "almost there" is so incredibly motivating because it triggers this constant, low-grade release of dopamine. The brain interprets visible progress as a signal that the hunt is going well, which in turn fuels our persistence and keeps us engaged in the effort.

When this cycle of progress and pursuit is happening within a **meaningful challenge** that perfectly balances our skills, we enter the optimal state of **Flow**. Flow is not a magical occurrence; it is the psychological experience of the dopamine-progress loop operating at peak efficiency. We have clear goals, we get immediate feedback that we are moving forward, and the challenge is just enough to keep the dopamine system firing, making the effort feel intrinsically rewarding.

Finally, this entire engine - from dopamine to progress to flow - operates in service of a unified theory of human needs: **Self-Determination Theory (SDT)**. SDT tells us that humans have an innate need for **Autonomy**, **Competence** (or Mastery), and **Relatedness**. The systems we've described are the machinery that fulfills those needs:

- The pursuit fueled by **dopamine** is the experience of **Autonomy** in action.

- The feedback from *The Progress Principle* builds our sense of **Competence**.

- When this occurs in a collaborative or supportive environment, it satisfies our need for **Relatedness**.

By understanding this nested model, we can now see that the most effective motivational systems are not those that simply offer rewards, but those that are designed to honor this entire sequence: from sparking the dopamine-driven hunt to creating the experience of progress, which fosters a state of flow and ultimately satisfies our deepest psychological needs.

This is the scientific foundation upon which the design principles in Part 3 are built. We are no longer just manipulating behavior; we are engineering for human thriving. But knowledge of the foundation is not enough. An architect can understand the principles of physics, but still needs a blueprint to build a skyscraper that stands. Part 3 provides that blueprint. It translates the *what* and the *why* of motivation into a practical, step-by-step *how*.

PART

THREE

EXECUTION

From Knowing to Designing

Welcome now to the part of the book where it gets challenging!

By now, the patterns should be clear.

You already understand why a lot of current approaches to motivation are falling short. You have seen how effort requires dopamine (Dr. Huberman: *"Dopamine is about wanting, not about having."),* how autonomy unlocks performance, and how (almost there) progress makes difficulty feel worthwhile. These are not mysteries anymore. They are known effects, backed by research and observed in the real world.

And yet, systems still fail.

The failure arises not because the science is wrong but because the design is missing. Many people understand the principles of motivation and speak about it with confidence, yet the step of actually building environments where motivation can take root is never taken.

This is the dangerous moment where even well-intentioned organizations stall. Insight turns into inertia. They host workshops. They write strategy decks. They roll out one more round of nudges or perks. The intention is there. The transformation is not.

Because knowing is not designing.

There is a widely held belief that runs beneath most business cultures. The assumption that once people are aware of what works, they will simply start doing it. Just hand them the principles. Just show them the benefits. The rest will fall into place.

It never does.

Because principles without architecture are just slogans.

You cannot out-inspire a broken system. You cannot out-communicate a structure that demotivates by design. You cannot drop science into a process map and expect magic to happen.

What you need is something else.

You need a method that connects the insight to the implementation. A way to move from understanding human motivation to building something that respects it. A system that does not just explain engagement but makes it unavoidable.

That is what this section is for.

The frameworks you are about to see are not abstract models. They are practical, modular, and built to be used together. They allow you to move from a vague sense of "we should make this more engaging" to a precise design sequence that actually works.

And once you see how it fits, you will not design the same way again.

DRIVE METHOD™: A ROADMAP TO MOTIVATION THAT LASTS

If motivation is simply about telling people what to do and offering a reward, the world would be full of high-performing systems. It is not.

The gap is not in effort. It is in architecture.

organizations do not struggle because they lack ambition. They struggle because they rely on what can be measured instead of what actually works. The spreadsheet gives them certainty. The people inside the spreadsheet give them chaos. That chaos, of course, is called human nature. And unless you build with it in mind, you will continue to fight it.

The *Drive Method* is how you stop fighting: it is not a theory, it is not a gimmick, it is a structured sequence for turning motivational insight into motivational infrastructure.

Let's overview its five steps:

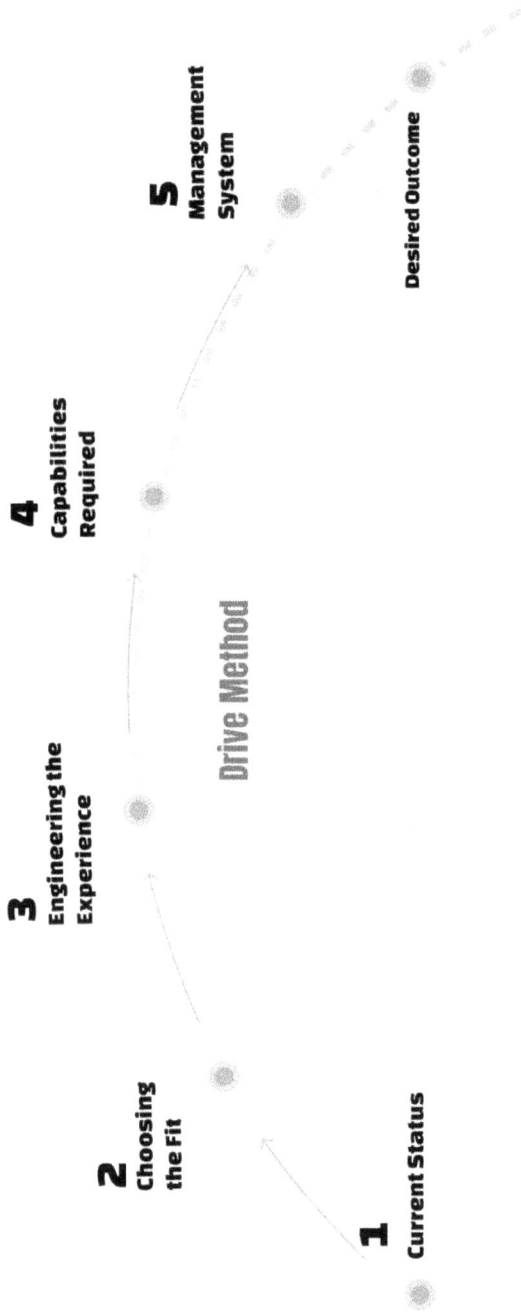

Figure 2: The Drive Method

Step 1: Current Status

What is actually happening?

This is where some people look at a problem only through the lens of logic: They point to KPIs, dashboards, and annual review scores. Then they ignore what people actually do when no one is looking.

If you are not brutally honest about the current state of motivation, everything else is cosmetic.

This step 1 concentrates on surfacing behavioral signals: not opinions, not aspirations, but signals. Where does motivation emerge on its own? Where does it die in contact with reality?

We are not diagnosing performance. We are diagnosing the current motivational design underneath it.

Step 2: Choosing the Fit

What type of motivation is actually need?

This is where most organizations guess. For example: They launch a new reward program for something that actually needs autonomy. Or they try to push intrinsic goals onto tasks that require precision and consistency, a behavior that is more effectively supported by extrinsic motivation.

This is where the core value of the *Behavioral Solution Matrix* shines.

Think of it as your decision compass. You map two things. First, the nature of the behavior you want to see, and therefore the motivation type required to get this behavior. Is it automatic or deliberate?

Second, the motivation type you are currently triggering.

Misalignment here is not just inefficient. It is destructive. Like asking for creative thinking while threatening quarterly penalties.

The matrix tells you what solution to use to get the required behavior.

Once you identify the right match, you stop wasting energy on strategies that feel smart in the boardroom but fail in the real world.

Step 3: Engineering the Experience

How to design for a less external (extrinsic) motivation type?

This is where our *IntrinsiQ Performance Journey* method shines.

The IntrinsiQ Performance Journey is the loop behind sustained engagement: a sequence of five psychological phases that turn a passing interest into long-term motivation.

This step 3 is where you stop hoping people will stay engaged as you design it so they do.

Step 4: Capabilities Required

What does the organization need to make this possible?

A motivational architecture, no matter how precise or well-designed, only becomes effective when the organization has the capacity to operate it. Not just once. Every day. Across contexts. With people. Otherwise the system remains conceptual.

This fourth step ensures that the motivational logic defined in step 3: *Engineering the Experience*, becomes a living part of the organization. It identifies what capabilities are required to bring the system to life and keep it running with integrity. This mainly involves the knowledge required to make such a design work effectively and sustainably. You need this knowledge within your organization in order to be effective.

Step 5: Management System

How do we keep it alive, adaptive, and credible?

Most engagement programs don't fail at launch; they decay silently, dying a slow death in the basement of forgotten initiatives.

Sustainability is not about repetition, but relevance.

You need a mechanism for observing how the system behaves over time. Where the motivational signals fade. Where friction returns. Where people start saying one thing and doing another.

The management system is not a performance review. It is the feedback loop that tells you when the motivational infrastructure needs recalibration.

Without this, you are driving blind.

These 5 steps from the Drive Method are your guidelines. Now let's dive deeper into each step of the overview and fill it with content.

1

Current Status

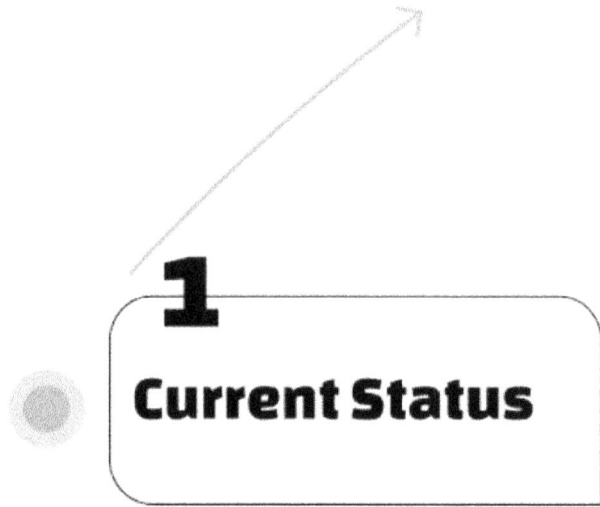

Figure 3: The Drive method - Step 1

Drive Method™ Detailed Manual

Step 1: Current Status

The first step of the Drive Method is a structured diagnostic that makes motivation visible and measurable. We don't guess. We analyze.

What this Step Uncovers

Here are examples of what we are really diagnosing:

- Are we asking people to be creative, but measuring them like factory workers?

- Do we expect proactive behavior in a system that punishes deviation?

- Is a learning process framed as a compliance task?

- Are leaders trying to spark ownership in an environment that blocks autonomy?

This work does not just highlight gaps. It shows the nature of the mismatch. For example:

- If the required motivation is *integrated* (see info box: The Six Motivation Types), but the system only supports *external* control, you will see short-term compliance, maybe even disengagement.

- If the task requires autonomy and mastery, but the environment produces *introjected* motivation (guilt, pressure), you will see passive resistance, presenteeism, and superficial engagement.

This is often less of a "people problem." It is more likely to be a system problem.

We create two profiles here:

The Required Motivation: What kind of motivation is *actually needed* for the behavior to be sustainable and high-quality?

The Supported Motivation: What kind of motivation is *currently being enabled* by the system, environment, culture, or tools?

Before you continue, revisit the Info Box 'The Six Motivation Types' to refresh the basics. You find it in the chapter: *Myth 8: Intrinsic Motivation is always the Goal.*

If the two overlap, we are in a good zone. If they don't, we have misalignment. And misalignment means friction, inefficiency, disengagement: compensatory mechanisms like over-monitoring, micromanagement, or increasing use of similar incentives.

Materials:

Key questions we ask in the diagnosis:

A. What kind of behavior is required for the particular job-to-be-done?

- Is it repetitive execution or adaptive problem-solving?
- Does it demand creative judgment, initiative, or procedural reliability?

B. What kind of motivation is required for that behavior to be sustained?

- Will extrinsic rewards drive it without compromising quality?
- Does the behavior require emotional buy-in or identity-level integration?
- Is the outcome best served by self-regulation, collaboration, or exploration?

C. What kind of motivation is currently being produced by the environment?

- What does the current reward system reinforce?
- Are signals aligned with progress, learning, and mastery?
- Is autonomy enabled or blocked?
- Are people acting out of pressure, obligation, or genuine interest?

This is not a simple survey to be completed at one's convenience. We treat it like a forensic analysis of cues, structures, rituals, narratives, and reinforcement mechanisms.

Outcome of Step 1

The goal is to answer one critical question with full clarity:

Is the current environment producing the type of motivation that matches the behavior we actually need?

If the answer is yes, the system can be scaled.

If not, we have the justified basis to go forward to adjust the conditions and rules, or to stop the initiative altogether and address the motivational misfit first. Because only when we know what kind of motivational architecture is needed (and also supported by the management) can we make the necessary decisions in Step 2.

Example - part 1: Why the Tool Must Match the Terrain

A global engineering company wanted to improve cross-team collaboration. In the past, a leaderboard was used to show who had added the most information to the system.

However the audit showed the desired behavior of proactive knowledge-sharing, which requires *integrated motivation*. The current environment only supported introjected or external motivation (pressure to contribute, fear of being left behind).

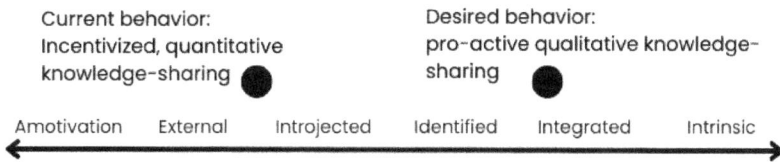

Current behavior:
Incentivized, quantitative
knowledge-sharing ●

Desired behavior:
pro-active qualitative knowledge-sharing ●

Amotivation   External   Introjected   Identified   Integrated   Intrinsic

---

Once we've identified a motivational misalignment in Step 1 (when the actual present motivation type does not match the required motivation type), the next move is to select the correct behavioral design tool to resolve it.

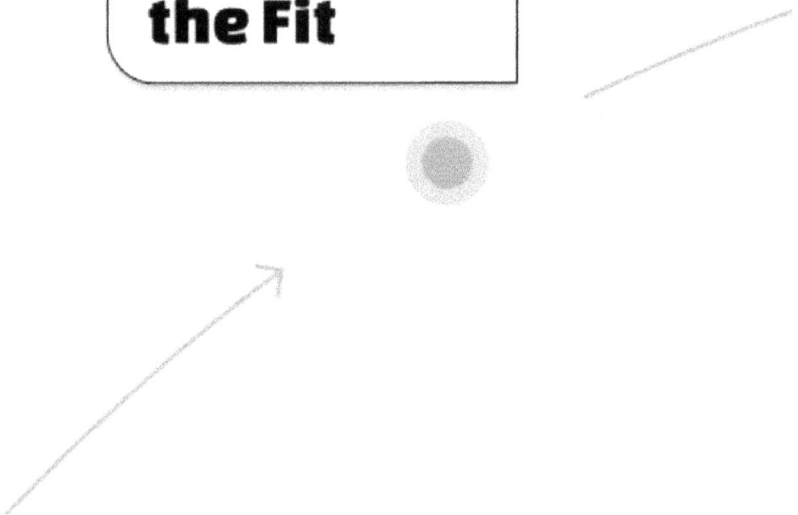

Figure 4: The Drive method - Step 2

Step 2: Choosing the Fit

To bridge the motivational gap, you need a structured way to match the right tool to the right problem. This requires a decision compass that I call the Behavioral Solution Matrix™

This Matrix comes with two axes:

- **Horizontal axis:** the Self-Determination Theory (SDT) motivation types (from amotivation to intrinsic)

- **Vertical axis:** the nature of the solution design (from highly implicit to highly explicit)

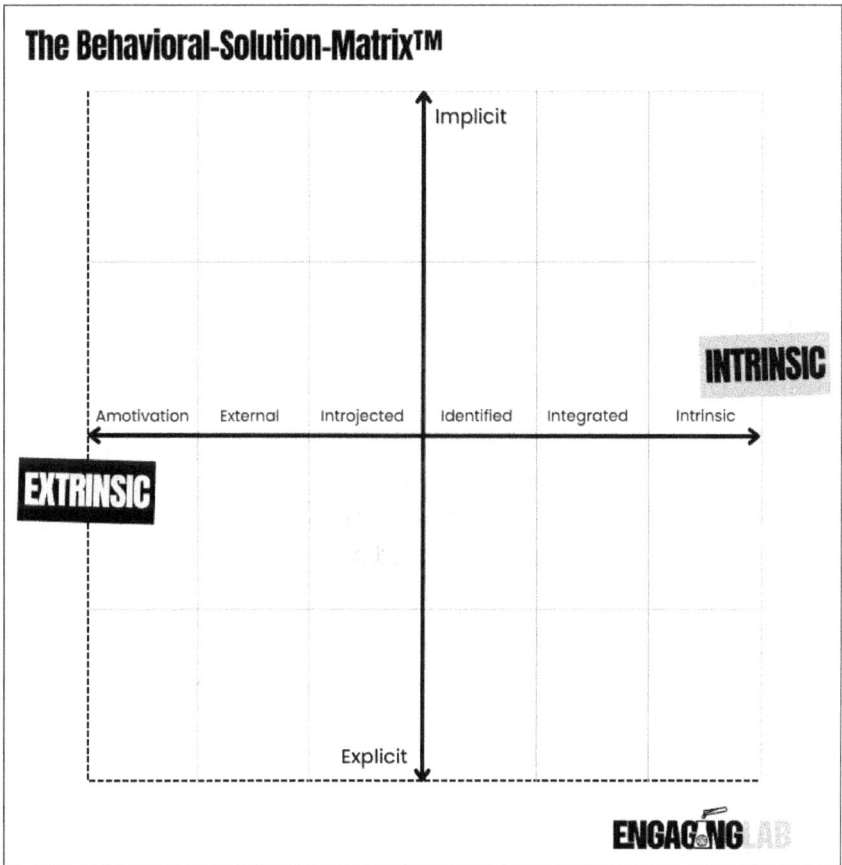

Figure 5: Behavioral Solution Matrix™

Info box: Explicit vs Implicit Design

When designing for motivation, you're not just choosing *what* to change. You're choosing *how visible* your intervention should be.

This is the difference between explicit and implicit design tools.

Explicit Design Tools

These are the obvious ones. They announce themselves to the user and shape behavior through clear structure, expectations, and consequences. They rely on visibility and deliberate decision-making.

Think:

- Reward programs
- Bonus structures
- Checklists
- Training sessions
- Leaderboards
- Penalty systems
- Public praise or recognition walls

Implicit Design Tools

- These are the subtle interventions. They guide behavior without needing to explain themselves. Often, people do not even notice them at play. But they shape action through friction, framing, feedback, and social cues.

Think:

- Smart defaults
- Nudges
- Progress bars
- Contextual prompts
- Visual hierarchy in interfaces
- Narrative cues in gamified journeys
- Environmental triggers (like music, layout, or timing)

Explicit design tools work well when the goal is clear, standardized, and outcome-focused. Think of repetitive tasks, compliance steps, or production-line activities. Their biggest advantage is clarity. People know what to do, how to do it, and what happens if they don't. But this clarity comes at a cost. Overuse can feel rigid, controlling, or transactional. They work, but only if the task itself is mechanical and the motivation does not need to last beyond the next step.

Implicit design tools shine in activity-focused environments where the path is less defined and the value emerges through the process. This includes creativity, problem-solving, collaboration, and learning. Their power lies in how they shape experience without demanding constant attention. They support flow, emotional connection, and self-directed progress. The downside? They are easy to overlook and harder to measure. But when used well, they make the desired behavior feel natural, even enjoyable.

In short:
Use **explicit tools** (e.g., user awareness, overt labeling, connection to formal rewards) when people need structure.[36]
Use **implicit tools** (e.g., shaping behavior below the level of conscious awareness, environmental cues, friction reduction) when people need space.[37]

The Matrix is not about judgement, but alignment.

From our experiences, every behavioral design tool carries its own motivational signature. It is effective in certain zones of the matrix, and less effecitve in others.

Each tool we work with has some kind of research- and experience-based position within the matrix. Based on my almost two decades of experience, I usually come across 16 instruments for behavioral interventions:

Info box: Some Well-Known Behavioral Design Interventions

1. Nudges

Example: Placing healthy foods at eye level in cafeterias.

2. Default Settings

Example: Automatic enrollment in retirement savings plans.

3. Framing

Example: Describing meat as "90% lean" instead of "10% fat."

4. Social Proof

Example: Telling hotel guests that "most people reuse their towels."

5. Commitment Devices

Example: Apps that lock your phone until you've completed a task.

6. Feedback Loops

Example: Smart meters showing energy usage in real time.

7. Loss Aversion

Example: Deposit contracts for weight loss: lose the weight or lose your money.

8. Attention Design

Example: Brightly colored reminders for medication adherence.

9. Simplification

Example: Streamlined forms or limited menu choices.

10. Timely Prompts

Example: Text reminders for appointments or medication.

11. Reward programs

Example: Applying points, prizes or badges to increase outcome orientated behavior.

12. Competition

Example: Using leaderboards, group goals, or friendly competition to drive behavior

13. Personalized Messaging

Example: Tailoring interventions to individual preferences, habits, or contexts to increase relevance and impact.

14. Positive Externalities

Example: Bringing in homemade lunch to eat healthier, and a colleague thanks you because it inspired them to stop ordering fast food and start meal prepping too.

15. Counter-Nudges

Example: On a social media app, after 15 minutes of continuous scrolling, the feed begins to blur slightly and display a message: "Still finding this valuable?" to trigger disengagement by disrupting flow and prompting self-reflection.

16. Value Reframing

Example: Highlighting that staying late at work every night is seen by high performers as poor time management, making this behavior feel less admirable, despite previously being recognised as hardworking.

17. Gamification

Example: A personal growth platform lets users pick a custom challenge path like "Explorer," "Craftsman," or "Mentor". Each one equipped with meaningful milestones that align with their goals and values.

Some tools operate well in environments that support extrinsic motivation. Others only generate traction if the system allows for autonomy, internalization, or intrinsic curiosity. Some are great hybrids and 'live in between'.

If you pick the wrong tool for the wrong motivational gap, even the best design will fail. Doing the wrong thing perfectly is a recipe for expensive failure.

That's what Step 2 prevents. In the matrix below, I show you an example of how I often categorise these different tools based on my experience.

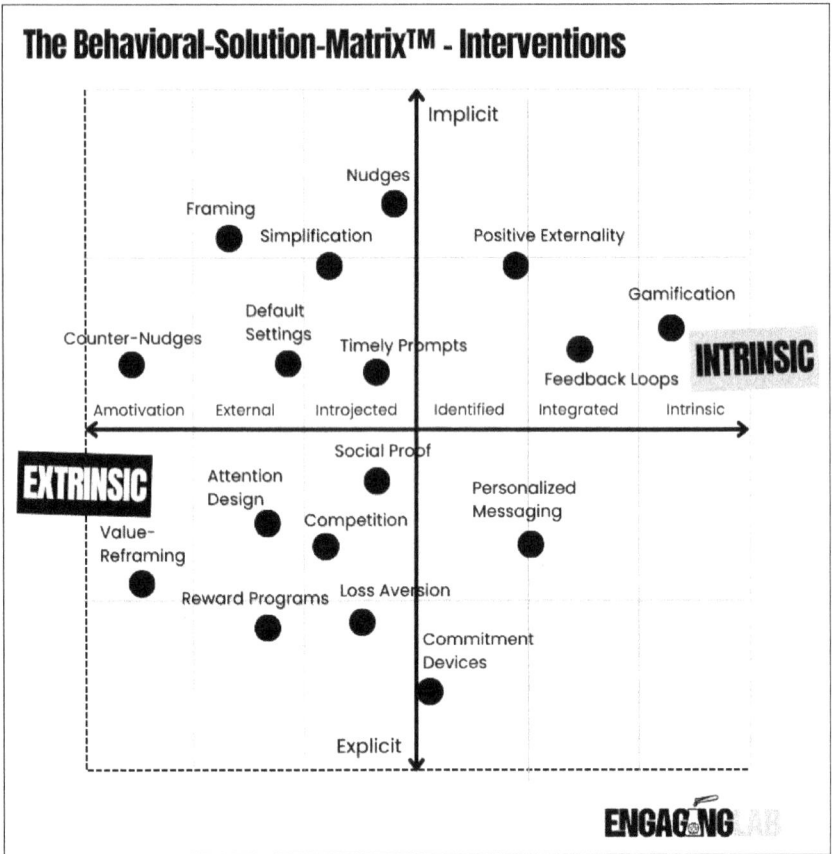

The Behavioral-Solution-Matrix™ - Interventions

Figure 6: The Behavioral Solution Matrix™ - Interventions

Info box: How a Tool is Placed in a Specific Quadrant

A rigid ruleset does not exist, telling you where to find each individual tool set in the matrix. I wish it were different, but we are moving in an area here that is not really deterministic.

The categorization of the tools in the matrix above is based on my experience from projects and, of course, the findings from scientific publications and how it has been successfully implemented.

For example: Nudges are placed in the implicit/external zone because they shape behavior without requiring conscious awareness (implicit) and are initiated by the environment, not the self (external regulation).

In contrast, a personalized mastery dashboard is placed in the implicit/intrinsic zone because it provides subtle feedback (implicit) that supports an individual's internal drive for competence and growth (intrinsic motivation).

Tool Selection: A Strategic Matchmaking Process

At this stage, we go back to the required motivational profile defined in Step 1.

- For a particular job-to-be-done, the desired behavior requires *identified motivation* (ownership over goals, but guided by external context)

- The current system supports mainly *external regulation* (rewards, control, competition)

- The motivational gap (from external to identified/integrated) needs to be closed without destabilizing operational reliability

Now we scan the design tools that operate in that transformation corridor. The matrix shows us:

- Which tools help to **transition** from the current motivation type to the desired one

Quick Start Heuristic:

For simple, repetitive tasks needing reliable compliance, start by exploring tools on the *explicit/external* side of the matrix. For complex, creative tasks needing deep ownership and innovation, start by exploring tools on the *implicit/intrinsic* side.

> **Example - part 2: Why the Tool Must Match the Terrain**
>
> A global engineering firm wanted to create more cross-team collaboration. They were tempted to use leaderboard-based Gamification because it looked dynamic and data-driven.
>
> However the audit showed the desired behavior of proactive knowledge-sharing requires *integrated motivation*. The current environment only supported introjected or external motivation (pressure to contribute, fear of being left behind).
>
> So, we used the matrix to rule out leaderboard mechanics as they would reinforce the wrong behavior and deepen the gap.
>
> Instead, we selected:
>
> - A symbolic impact system based on peer validation (**social proof**)
> - Autonomy-signaling mechanism embedded in weekly cycles (**feedback-loops**)
> - Mastery progress dashboard system that remained private, not public (**Gamification**)
>
> These tools had the right motivational signature. They worked within the psychological landscape of the teams and produced movement (transition) in the intended direction.

That's what this second step is also about: *tool-fit*, not wishful thinking.

We are not inventing solutions here. We are aligning available levers with the motivational transformation we now understand deeply.

Decision Output of Step 2

In the end, we know:

Which behavioral design tool (or combination) will create the motivational shift required to support the desired behavior in this particular context, for the target group, in a particular environment.

This is the moment where intention becomes direction. We move from theory to architecture.

Only after this foundation has been finished, does it make sense to begin the design phase.

That's what we do next in Step 3.

3
Engineering the Experience

Figure 7: The Drive method - Step 3

Step 3: Engineering the Experience

By now we have completed steps 1 and 2 of the Drive Method. We know where the motivational gap sits in the Behavioral Solution Matrix and which behavioral design tools could close it.

If the diagnosis places the situation on the left side of the matrix, meaning amotivation, external regulation, or introjected regulation, the Drive Method effectively concludes here. In these cases established operational tools are appropriate. Use clear incentives, constraints, defaults, training, checklists, and environment tweaks. These solutions are well known and are not the focus of this book.

If the analysis points to identified regulation, integrated regulation, or intrinsic motivation, we proceed with Step 3. In this case the behavior we want to support requires an experience that cultivates ownership and meaning. We therefore turn to the IntrinsiQ Performance Journey™, a framework designed to build identified, integrated, and intrinsic motivation in practice.

This framework aligns with the non-Skinnerian school of thought that has guided our work. If you want a refresher on how I differentiate between classic gamification and non-Skinnerian gamification, please revisit the related info box from Section 1.

The IntrinsiQ Performance Journey™

At its core, the *IntrinsiQ Performance Journey* is a structured experience design based on five principles: *curiosity, interest, positive externality, autonomy, and mastery.* This means that motivation is no longer just a product of chance, but a property of the system.[38] People do not develop because they are pushed by others with rational arguments. They develop because the structure of their environment invites and enables them to do so. Motivation becomes less a question of willpower and more a function of design.[39]

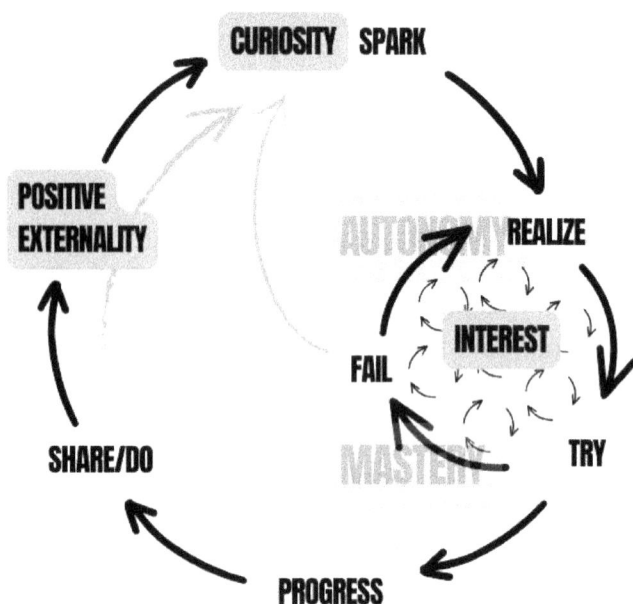

Figure 8: The IntrinsiQ™ Performance Journey Loop

Each of the five steps activates a distinct psychological mechanism. When they are present and sequenced well, people enter a motivational loop. One that reinforces itself. One that grows stronger each time it is repeated. And one that aligns fully with how the human brain is wired for performance, discovery, and contribution.

Let us walk through each step.

Step 1: Curiosity

Trigger exploration without pressure.

At this stage, we create entry points that spark spontaneous interest. Not through instruction, but through invitation. These are often symbolic, social, or contextual cues that make something worth investigating.

x

CURIOSITY SPARK

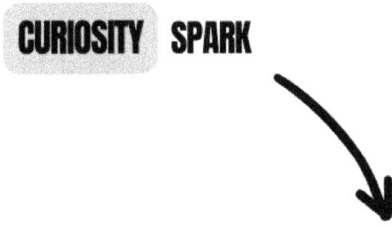

Figure 9: IntrinsiQ™ Loop - Step 1: Curiosity

Design actions:

- Use unexpected artifacts, information or signals to spark interest

- Embed discoverable content or choices that reward initiative

- Create low-friction first interactions with meaningful micro-surprises

- Avoid over-explaining, allow ambiguity to generate pull.

This is the opposite of onboarding with mandatory tutorials. Curiosity is created through strategic withholding, not information overload. What we learned in the past is that often this can be achieved by removing rituals, policies or structures that are responsible for monotony or indifference from the actual situation. So, sometimes design is not just about adding something from the outside to motivate, but to remove something that is already there.

Examples:

In a **sales onboarding** process, instead of starting with product specs, you might pose a question. "Why do 90 percent of our biggest deals follow a completely different sales pattern than the rest?" That puzzle is not just content. It is a hook. And if you don't know the answer to this, it becomes an invitation for exploration.

In compliance training, instead of beginning with a list of rules, you might start with a real incident.

"Last year, one of our most experienced team members unknowingly triggered a security breach. He followed the rules but still caused a failure. Can you spot where the system failed him?" This reframes compliance as a mystery to be solved, not a checklist to be memorized.

In product onboarding, rather than launching into features, open with a challenge: "Before you explore what this platform can do, here's something we've seen: 70 percent of users make the same mistake in their first week. Can you avoid it?" Now you have attention. Not because the tool is flashy, but because the user wants to prove they're not part of the 70 percent.

In leadership development, rather than listing leadership traits, pose a social puzzle: "Which leadership trait do people say they value most, but almost always punish when they see it in action?" This turns leadership into a cognitive dissonance challenge. Curiosity is no longer optional. It is personal.

In **customer education or loyalty programs**, rather than showcasing benefits immediately, begin with a question: "Why do our most loyal customers buy less frequently than everyone else, and yet deliver three times the value?" This invites rethinking, not obedience. Curiosity becomes the entry into a deeper brand relationship.

In **internal communications or culture rollouts** start with a contradiction: "Last quarter, 80 percent of employees said they feel 'highly productive.' But only 27 percent said they know what actually moves the company forward. What is going on?" You do not need to have the answer yet. The tension is the point. People lean in to resolve the gap.

Psychological function: This stage activates the brain's reward system through dopamine release, not because of achievement, but because of the *possibility* of progress. Remember: dopamine does not fire when we receive a reward. It fires when we sense something meaningful *might* be around the corner.

Common mistake to avoid: organizations try to motivate by providing information instead of sparking interest. They start with lectures instead of questions. They kill curiosity by front-loading the answer.

Step 2: Interest and Progress

Transform attention into personal relevance.

Once attention is sparked, it must be stabilized. Interest arises when the individual begins to feel that it is worth following the initial curiosity trigger. Perhaps one curiosity spark leads to another while someone is trying to make sense out of the first one.

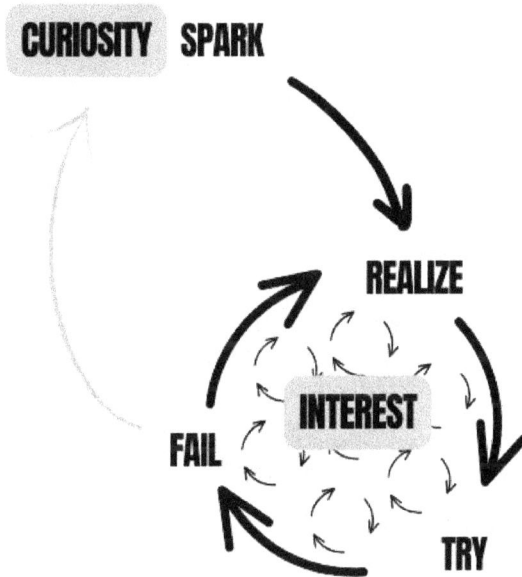

Figure 10: IntrinsiQ™ Loop - Steps 2: Interest

Design actions:

- Reveal structure and progression without overwhelming detail
- Introduce internal logic: why this, why now, what for

- Allow small wins that unlock feedback loops and spark confidence

- Frame activities in the user's language, not institutional jargon

At this stage, feedback is layered in not to control, but inform. Interest grows when interaction becomes personally interpretable.

Examples:

The Insight Threadboard - B2B Commerce

We introduced a physical and digital wall that highlights real but unexplained patterns from business operations and customer behavior. Each entry includes minimal initial data and the date it was logged, such as "This client behavior changed without explanation." Team members can subscribe to threads, contribute observations, and build on each other's hypotheses over time. What began as isolated anomalies developed into shared intellectual puzzles. Some threads led to internal case studies, others to process improvements. The system turned ambiguity into a catalyst for cross-functional learning and made curiosity part of our daily workflow.

The Incompleteness Dashboard - Consumer Goods Brand

For an organization selling household goods we designed key systems to signal intentional incompleteness rather than perfection. Dashboards now highlight missing pieces, such as metrics without clear ownership. Workflows include prompts that ask for suggestions when a task is functional but lacks meaning. Presentations often end by naming what remains uncertain or unsolved. This approach encourages people to step in where they see gaps. It activates thoughtful engagement and invites contribution without relying on external rewards. Over time, it has helped build a culture where problem-solving begins with recognizing what is still unknown.

> **Hidden Architecture Maps - Administration department**
>
> For a company that provides complex and highly regulated services, we created multi-layered documentation across product, IT and compliance areas that only reveals deeper structures when actively explored. Starting from a product interface, users can trace links to process logic, legal justification and the original business rationale. Each level becomes visible through editing rather than passive browsing. New employees and analysts follow these paths to understand why certain elements exist. Over time, this has transformed complex legacy systems into navigable landscapes that inspire a deeper understanding and sustained interest in how things are structured and why they matter.

Psychological function: This phase amplifies the dopamine feedback loop. Progress becomes the reward. Novelty continues to fire curiosity. The brain begins to associate the activity with competence, growth, and momentum.

Common mistake to avoid: Systems rush to outcomes. They flatten exploration into bullet points. They remove all friction, hoping to make it "easy," and in doing so, remove the feeling of growth.

Step 3: Positive Externality

Make impact visible beyond the self.

This is where a lot of motivation gets reinforced. People stay engaged when they see that their effort creates a ripple effect that leads to changes in the system, in others or in themselves.

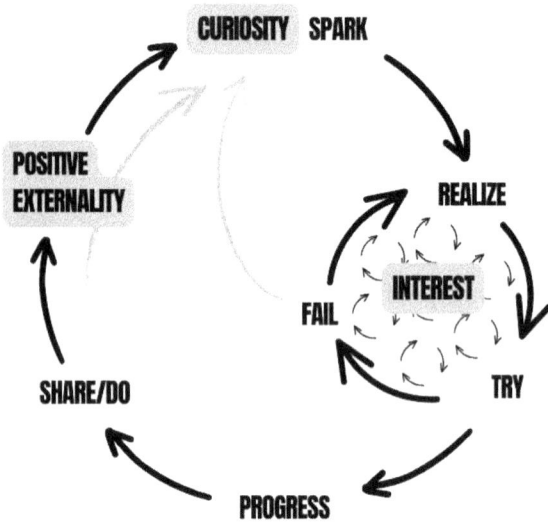

Figure 11: IntrinsiQ™ Loop - Step 3: Positive Externality

Design actions:

- Make contributions visible to others in authentic ways
- Connect actions to team, customer, or systemic outcomes
- Trigger positive feedback signals that feel earned, not granted
- Design social reinforcement that celebrates progress, not status

This is a very common pitfall in gamification design. If the impact becomes competitive or forced, the motivation shifts from internal to image-driven.

Examples:

Ripple Feed - IT

For an IT-development company we introduced a ripple feed that quietly reflects the real-world impact of meaningful actions across the organization. When someone makes a contribution, such as a designer refactoring a shared component, the system generates a subtle update like "Your update improved load times across six active projects." These acknowledgments appear without likes or reactions. They are not broadcast to others, but shown directly to the contributor. The aim is not to celebrate for applause, but to reinforce the quiet satisfaction that comes from knowing one's work creates tangible benefits beyond the self. Over time, this has helped shift focus from recognition to resonance.

Upstream-Downstream Visuals - HR

An engineering company asked to create a more inherent onboarding program. We introduced upstream-downstream visuals to help people see how their individual actions contribute to meaningful outcomes for others. During onboarding, new employees are shown how careful data entry leads to faster approvals for applicants, which in turn reduces stress for young families. These connections are presented as simple, cause-and-effect sequences that link internal tasks to external impact. Especially in bureaucratic or complex systems, where results are often abstract or delayed, this approach makes contribution tangible. It helps individuals understand that their attention to detail is not just efficient but genuinely valuable to real people.

Shared Progress Moments - SaaS

Following a request from a company to provide cooperation on internal competition, we began highlighting shared progress moments to celebrate milestones that were only possible through the quiet, distributed efforts of many. One update read, "Week twelve: Thanks to nine micro-fixes across teams, our platform uptime just crossed 99.95 percent. This was no one's job. But it became everyone's win." These moments are not tied to individual recognition but to a collective sense of achievement. They show how progress often emerges from uncoordinated yet aligned contributions. Over time, this prac-

tice has helped build a deeper sense of co-ownership and quiet pride in shared outcomes.

Psychological function: This activates oxytocin and vasopressin, which strengthen social bonds and purpose. As the brain
shifts from individual gain to group contribution we feel connected, needed, and useful.

Common mistake to avoid: Systems often isolate learners. By
viewing learning as an individual journey, they miss the oppor-
tunity to celebrate progress as a community.

Step 4: Autonomy

Enable meaningful choices with real consequences.

Autonomy in this loop is not freedom for its own sake. It is the
feeling of agency within a meaningful structure. Participants
should experience that their decisions matter, and that they
shape the journey.

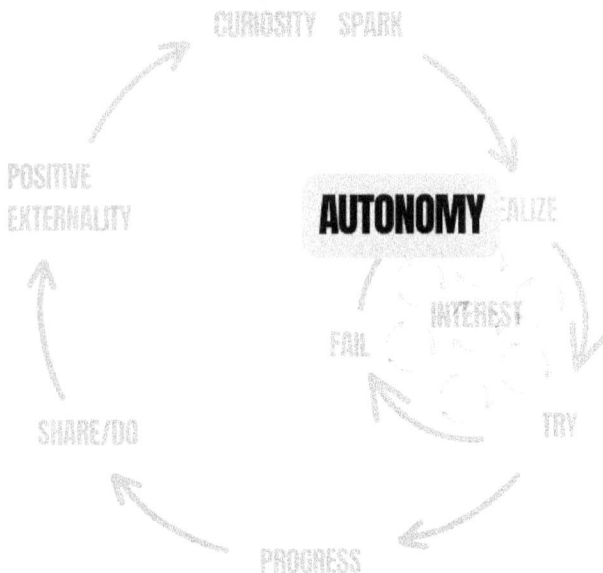

Figure 12: IntrinsiQ™ Loop - Step 4: Autonomy

Design actions:

- Create possibilities for branching paths or multiple pro-gression modes

- Allow role definition or tool selection based on personal strategy

- Enable adjustments to goal-setting based on decisions at work

- Make mistakes recoverable and part of the growth loop

The presence of choice is not enough. The stakes of choice must be real. This is where systems shift from simple engagement to ownership.

Examples:

Branching Ownership Paths - Product Development

Especially in daily tasks that quickly become routine, the feeling of autonomy diminishes fast. This is why we introduced branching ownership paths to let contributors decide how they wanted to support a shared goal. In one product team, members could choose whether to focus on stability, speed, or innovation sprints. Each path came with its own set of metrics, timelines, and expectations. Over time, we reflected on how these choices shaped user outcomes and team dynamics. This made individual decisions visible and meaningful, showing that different contributions were not just valid but strategically important. Autonomy became more than flexibility. It became a way for people to see the real consequences of their direction.

Personal Strategy Declaration - Sales team

We introduced personal strategy declarations to give pharmaceutical sales professionals a stronger sense of authorship in how they approach their territories. During onboarding, each team member is invited to define their own strategic focus. This way, a representative can choose to prioritize long-term physician education over short-term prescription volume. Six months later, a review traces how this approach leads to deeper relationships with key accounts and more consistent en-

---

gagement across touchpoints. The reflection is not about ranking performance but about showing how individual strategy influences trust, retention, and regional outcomes. It helps to shift the mindset from executing a sales role to actively shaping how that role creates value.

Long-View Decision Trail - HR Department

As part of the effort to improve the overall employee lifecycle for a software services company, we introduced a long-view decision trail within major transformation projects. The goal was to help people see their long-term impact and understand how their decisions shape the organization's trajectory and their own. In a two-year initiative, every major directional change was recorded with clear attribution and a brief explanation of the reasoning behind it. This created a transparent timeline that employees could revisit to see how their choices influenced outcomes over time. It helped move beyond task execution toward narrative authorship, giving people a deeper sense of ownership. By making contributions visible across the full arc, we reinforced the idea that each individual's strategic thinking plays a lasting role in the company's evolution. This shift supported a more meaningful employee experience across onboarding, development, and retention.

Psychological function: Autonomy reduces cortisol and triggers intrinsic motivation. When people feel they are *choosing* their actions, they are more committed to the outcome.

Common mistake: Leaders try to maintain control. They prescribe every step, robbing the learner of ownership. The result is compliance, not commitment.

5. Mastery

Show growth. Celebrate depth.

Mastery is the emotional payoff of the whole loop. It is when individuals begin to recognize their own transformation, not only in outcome, but in self-perception.

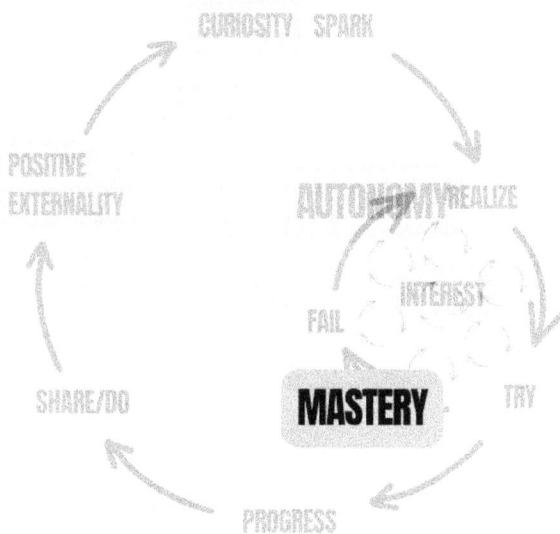

Figure 13: IntrinsiQ™ Loop - Step 5: Mastery

Design actions:

- Install clear long-term patterns of progress

- Make skill or insight visible through accumulation, not comparison

- Introduce reflection mechanisms that highlight personal evolution

- Enable contribution back into the system, becoming a signal to others

Mastery must feel earned, not granted. It closes the loop and invites the next cycle, but now from a higher baseline of confidence and clarity.

Examples:

Quiet Mastery Signals - Employee Retention program

To help an organization prove to their employees that it was a good decision to join them in the first place, and it makes sense to stay, we introduced quiet mastery signals into their internal systems to make depth of contribution visible. In a design platform, each contributor's profile now highlights areas where they have made layered input over time. One example shows that a team member has revised six design principles since 2022. There is no leaderboard, no comparison, and no public ranking. The focus is on showing thoughtful accumulation rather than frequency or volume. This subtle shift helped people see themselves not just as contributors, but as stewards of evolving knowledge. It affirmed that long-term engagement and careful refinement are valued just as much as bold innovation.

Mastery Progress Maps - Customer Retention program

To enable customers to recognize their own growth while learning and applying our client's complex software, we introduced transformation milestone journals supported by a visual spiderweb diagram. Their feature usage is paired with a spiderweb chart that shows visible progress across key skill sets, such as data interpretation, workflow configuration, and scenario modeling. This diagram updates with each reflection cycle, helping users see how their capabilities expand over time. It turns the experience from a learning curve into a mastery journey. The software becomes not just a tool, but a catalyst for personal development, and users begin to see their investment as part of a growing, long-term skill profile.

The DIY Skill Tree - Loyalty program

We developed a progress tree loyalty program for a DIY building store brand to help customers see how their skills grow as they take on new projects. Each branch represents a core area like measuring, cutting, assembling, or finishing. As customers complete real tasks using the store's tools or materials, new branches open up to suggest what they are ready for next. For example, after completing a basic shelving project, the tree might unlock a new challenge like mounting shelves on uneven walls. The tree expands with each experience, showing how far the customer has come. It turns home improvement into a visible journey of growing confidence and capability, all supported by the store's ecosystem

Psychological function: This stage engages endorphins and serotonin. It reinforces competence, builds confidence, and strengthens identity. People begin to see themselves as capable.

Common mistake to avoid: Mastery is treated as a finish line. But real mastery is a turning point. It should reveal new paths, not close the door.

Each phase of the journey directly corresponds to the satisfaction of one or more of the three core psychological needs identified by Deci and Ryan: Autonomy, Competence, and Relatedness.[14] The following table demonstrates this alignment:

Info box: Connection to The Self-Determination Theory (SDT)

IntrinsiQ Phase	Description	Primary SDT Need Fulfilled	Mechanism of Action
Curiosity & Interest	Trigger exploration and transform attention into personal relevance.	Competence & Autonomy	Creates a sense of agency. The initial feeling of 'figuring it out" satisfies the need for competence.
Positive Externality	Make impact visible beyond the self, connecting actions to team or systemic outcomes.	Relatedness	Fulfills the need to feel connected and contribute to something larger.

Autonomy	Enable meaningful choices with real consequences that shape the journey.	Autonomy	Directly satisfies the need to be the author of one's own actions. Shifts the locus of control from external to internal.
Mastery	Show growth, celebrate depth, and make skill progression visible.	Competence	Directly satisfies the need to feel effective and masterful.

The Power of the Loop

The *IntrinsiQ Performance Journey* is not a one-way track. It is a loop that builds strength through repetition. Every time someone completes it, their sense of agency increases. Their performance rises. Their attachment to the work deepens.

This is also why shortcuts fail.

You cannot decorate an activity with rewards and expect mastery. You cannot skip curiosity and start with goals. You cannot force autonomy after taking it away.

Each step matters. And each one makes the next possible.

This model works across contexts: onboarding, learning journeys, product experiences, even long-term transformation efforts. What matters is that the system follows the psychological rhythm of how humans *want* to engage when they are at their best.

Repetition Builds Bonding

Going through the loop once is helpful. But going through it multiple times is transformative.

Each complete cycle strengthens a person's emotional connection to the activity. Not because someone praised them. But because they felt something shift. They experienced progress. They saw meaning. They exercised autonomy. And they came out stronger.

This emotional bonding is what makes people stay engaged even when things get hard.

It creates *resilience*: the capacity to push through setbacks without giving up.

It builds *ownership*: the belief that this task, this role, this outcome is *mine*.

And it unlocks *peak performance*: not as an occasional burst, but as a repeated state, accessible through the right conditions.

organizations that build this kind of environment are not just more productive. They become cultural outliers. Their people give more. Solve harder problems. Care longer. Not because someone watches them. Because something inside them was activated and kept alive.

A System, Not a Speech

If your culture cannot be felt in the day-to-day experience of work, it is not real.

The *IntrinsiQ Performance Journey* provides the scaffolding for that experience. It shows you what to build and in what sequence, to make performance feel personal and purposeful again.

"This is not about motivating individuals. It is about designing contexts where motivation becomes the default."

If someone fails in your system, the first question should not be 'What is wrong with them?' It should be, 'Where did we break the loop?'.

Once that architecture exists, we move to the next step: Can the organization deliver it? Can it live and evolve inside the system and its constraints?

That is the work of Step 4 of the Drive Method.

4
Capabilities Required

Figure 14: The Drive method - Step 4

Step 4: Capabilities Required

Designing the right motivational system is essential. But it is not enough to survive when things get questioned.

A brilliant motivational architecture is useless without the organizational capacity to operate it. Not just once. Every day. Across contexts. Through real people. Without that, the system remains conceptual.

This step ensures that the motivational logic defined in *Engineering the Experience* becomes a living part of the organization. It identifies what capabilities are required to bring the system to life and keep it running with integrity.

What capabilities are required

Delivering and sustaining a motivational system requires more than management support. It requires specific operational capabilities. These are the five most critical:

1. **Behavioral design literacy**

   Do key people understand how motivation works?
   Can they recognize motivational signals and friction points?
   Are they able to distinguish between behavior, outcome, and intent?

2. **Signal and feedback competence**

   Are feedback loops active and meaningful?
   Can leaders and facilitators interpret behavioral signals in real time?
   Do they respond in ways that reinforce the right type of motivation?

3. **Autonomy-support infrastructure**

   Does the organization know how to enable meaningful choice without creating chaos?
   Is there a structure that allows participants to act with

ownership, not just permission?
Are people trained to guide rather than control?

4. Maintenance and iteration routines

Who is responsible for the ongoing care of the system?
Is there a process to gather insights, test adjustments, and improve the experience continuously?
Are cycles of review built into operational rhythm?

5. Cultural readiness

Does the organization accept that motivation is not a mindset problem but a system design issue?
Are leaders prepared to let go of control logic where it no longer serves?
Is there language in place to normalize experimentation and signal safety?

If these capabilities are missing, the system does not fade but it fails quietly and with it the old logic returns.

Let's say a company rolls out a new learning platform to boost employee skills and engagement. The platform is technically robust, but within a few months, participation drops off a cliff. Why? Because the critical capabilities weren't in place:

- **Behavioral design literacy:** The team running the platform doesn't really understand what motivates people to learn. They rely on generic incentives (badges, points) instead of building in real curiosity or relevance.

- **Signal and feedback competence:** There is no meaningful feedback. Employees complete modules but only receive automatic "Congratulations!" messages. They cannot recognize any effects or real consequences for their daily work afterwards.

- **Autonomy-support infrastructure:** The learning paths are rigid. Everyone must follow the same sequence, regardless of their interests or job needs. There's no room for choice, so people feel like passengers, not drivers.

- **Maintenance and iteration routines:** Once launched, the platform is left on autopilot. No one reviews usage data or asks for feedback, so problems go unnoticed and the experience never improves.

- **Cultural readiness:** Leadership sees the platform as a checkbox, not a living system. There's no encouragement for experimentation, and managers still micromanage learning time.

Result: The result is that employees quietly disengage. The platform sits unused. The company concludes that people just are not motivated, but in reality, the system was never designed to support motivation in the first place.

Takeaway: The lesson is clear. Even the most advanced tools will fail if you do not have the right capabilities to run them, adapt them, and nurture the environment around them. **Motivation is not a one-time fix; it is an ongoing practice that depends on the right foundation**.

Build. Train. Partner.

No company has all capabilities fully developed on day one. What matters is the decision to either build them internally, train the right people intentionally, or partner with experts who can operate the system while knowledge and maturity are growing.

This is not outsourcing. It is scaffolding. The goal is to make the system self-sustaining over time. But without these capabilities, even the best design will degrade quickly. Train the right people intentionally.

A cautionary example

A global learning initiative began with a carefully designed onboarding journey that closely followed the IntrinsiQ loop. The concept was strong, and early engagement was promising.

After the initial momentum, participation began to slow. Interaction dropped, feedback cycles fell apart, progress track-

---

ing stopped working, and employees grew uncertain. Teams slipped back into their old habits.

The issue did not lie in the core design. It came from a lack of operational capability. No one owned the program, there was no regular rhythm for feedback, the rituals were unclear, and the environment did not support what the concept required.

Once this capability gap was identified, the company realigned internal roles, trained team leads in behavioral feedback, and built in simple review routines. Engagement recovered, the system found its footing, and the change finally held.

The outcome of Step 4

What capabilities are required to operate the motivational system
Who will deliver or develop them
How they will be protected, supported, and maintained over time

Motivational systems are living systems. This fourth step ensures that they have what they need to survive and thrive inside a real organization.

Now we face the final piece of the Drive Method.

While step 4 is exclusively about people and skills, the final step is about processes and rituals.

How do we align this new motivational system with how performance is actually tracked, reinforced, and sustained across the business?

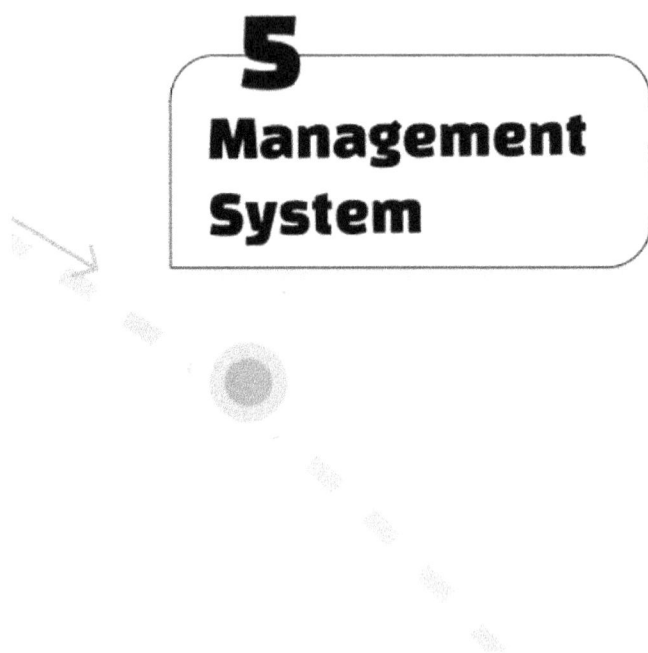

Figure 15: The Drive method - Step 5

Step 5: Management System

The final step in the Drive Method ensures that your new motivational system does not remain a side story.

Motivational systems run on behavior, emotion, progression, and internal commitment. Traditional management systems track output, goals, and results. If these systems remain disconnected, the motivational system is at risk.

It might work. But it will not count.

Step 5 ensures that your design can be measured, evaluated, and anchored in the organization's existing logic of recognition, promotion, and strategic relevance.

The Core Challenge: Two Logics at Work

You are now operate two systems that can coexist:

1. A **motivational architecture**, perhaps even structured along the IntrinsiQ Performance Journey, which supports curiosity, learning, collaboration, and mastery.
2. A **more traditional system**, typically built around targets, KPIs, financial outcomes, and quarterly cycles.

Both systems bring valuable strengths, even if they follow different logics. When thoughtfully aligned, they can reinforce one another rather than compete. Leaders learn to read and respond to new signals, and participants feel their efforts recognized across both dimensions. This alignment builds coherence, recognition, and ultimately deeper trust.

The Purpose of this Step

This fifth step is not about optimizing the motivational system. That was Step 3.

This step 5 is about making sure that what you built is:

- Recognized by leadership
- Evaluated in a way that fits its function

- Connected to the real systems of promotion, rewards, and prioritization

Motivational systems must be integrated into the language and rhythms of management.

If they are not, they are dismissed as soft, optional, or cosmetic.

Design Objectives for the Management Layer

This includes four strategic design tasks:

1. **Translate motivational signals into trackable indicators** Behavioral engagement must be made visible. But not through vanity metrics (surface-level numbers that look impressive but do not reflect meaningful progress or behavior change, for example likes, views, and clicks).

Use indicators like:

- Loop completion (not just task completion)

- Depth of participation (e.g. variation, reflection, autonomy use)

- Peer signaling (feedback initiated, not just received)

- Resilience over time (how engagement holds in challenging moments)

2. **Align motivational cycles with performance rhythms** Weekly sprints, quarterly reviews, and OKR cycles must accommodate the pace and feedback structure of the motivational design. That means:

- Integrating check-ins with progress indicators from the gamified system

- Reporting not only what was done, but how and why

- Framing performance reviews around mastery progression and decision quality, not only output volume

3. **Integrate into hierarchy, recognition, and promotion logic**
   If the motivational system builds behaviors the company says it values, then those behaviors must be reflected in:

- Promotion criteria

- Leadership development tracks

- Recognition systems

- Cross-functional visibility

- Without that, participants will quickly learn that intrinsic effort earns no real-world return.

4. **Create a long-term evaluation loop**
   Beyond quarterly reporting, create a cycle for evaluating the system itself:

- Is it still generating the right kind of motivation?

- Are the signals still resonant?

- Is the system producing positive second-order effects (collaboration, resilience, problem-solving capacity)?

This is how you evolve the system without diluting its core.

Translating Motivation into Management Logic

How to align motivational signals with traditional performance systems

Motivational System (e.g. Intrinsic Design Logic)	Performance Management System (Outcome Logic)
Completion of full IntrinsiQ Performance Journey loop cycles	Completion of tasks, delivery of milestones
Evidence of autonomous decision-making	Achievement of predefined targets
Voluntary engagement beyond required participation	Attendance, compliance, and throughput
Initiated peer feedback or contribution to others' learning	Formal evaluations or team lead feedback

Visible progression in personal challenge level or role complexity	Static job role performance or quarterly output metrics
Signals of identity alignment and long-term ownership	Tenure, role retention, or loyalty indicators
Reflection rituals and self-evaluation completed	External performance review and manager assets
Behavior under ambiguity or challenge (resilience)	Crisis performance or problem resolution under time pressure
Skill layering over time (visible mastery curves)	Certification or formal qualification completion
Self-generated learning loops or initiative taking	Strategic project contributions or process improvements

Final Thought: Visibility is Protection

Sometimes motivational systems fail not because they stop working but because they remain invisible to decision-makers. They are excluded from dashboards, ignored in strategy, and misunderstood in reviews.

It is the responsibility of this step 5 to fix that.

It builds the bridge between motivational quality and operational legitimacy, and once that bridge is built, the motivational system becomes more than a program.

It becomes part of how the organization defines excellence.

Section 3 Wrap-Up

At the beginning of this section, we introduced the core challenge that most organizations face when trying to improve performance or just doing the best they can: They focus on symptoms instead of systems, they add tactics before understanding motivation, they optimize for results while misaligning the behavior required to achieve them.

What followed was a structured method to solve this problem at its root.

The Drive Method is not a theory. It is a repeatable, diagnostic-to-delivery system that aligns context with behavior and motivation in five deliberate steps:

Step 1: Diagnose the Current Status

We reveal the motivational misalignment between the behavior the organization needs and the type of motivation its current environment supports.

Step 2: Choose the Right Design Approach

We use the *Behavioral Solution Matrix* to map available behavioral design tools. We select the one that is capable of closing the motivational gap without creating new friction or breakdowns. This is where intention becomes direction.

Step 3: Engineering the Experience

Here we design the motivational system itself. In the example used in this section, the result pointed us toward Gamification, guided by the *IntrinsiQ Performance Journey*. Each phase of the loop - curiosity, interest, positive externality, autonomy, and mastery - becomes a design lens. What we build here is not a product or a feature, but a subjective experience of meaningful engagement.

Step 4: Capabilities Required

No system works without the operational ability to run it. It surfaces the behavioral, managerial, and cultural capabilities that must exist to bring the system to life.

Step 5: Management System

Every system, also a motivational system, must be recognized by the operational logic of the business. This fifth step integrates the new motivational signals into the organization's rhythm of performance reviews, KPIs, and promotion paths. It protects the system from irrelevance by making it visible, measurable, and legitimate.

Together, these five steps deliver what most transformation initiatives promise, but rarely achieve:

Clarity. Fit. Ownership. Scalability.
And above all: coherence between what an organization expects and what it actually enables.

The Drive Method is not about surface engagement. It is about systemic motivation.
It is built to make invisible behavioral dynamics measurable. It turns intention into architecture and it aligns performance with the psychological and social reality of human beings at work.

This is the moment where motivation stops being a talking point and becomes infrastructure.

Because once you can design motivation, you can design the future of your company.

NOW EXECUTE

Congratulations. You've reached the end, which means you've absorbed a dense and often counter-intuitive model for understanding human motivation. The real challenge, however, doesn't lie in understanding these ideas, but in applying them. The gap between knowing and doing is where most transformations fail.

This afterword is not an ending. It's a bridge. It's designed to provide you with two final pieces of value: a simple first step you can take on Monday morning and a complete case study showing how these frameworks connect in the real world.

Your First Move: A 15-Minute Signal Audit

Let's make this easy. You don't need a budget, a team, or permission to begin. All you need is 15 minutes and a new way of seeing.

Tomorrow, pick one routine process in your team, e.g., a weekly meeting, a project update email, a performance dashboard. Don't try to fix it. Just observe. Ask yourself one question:

"What behavior is this system *silently* rewarding?"

_____

_____

_____

Does it reward speed over thoughtfulness? Individual visibility over team collaboration? Speaking up over listening? Does it reward perfect-looking reports over honest, messy progress?

Write down the signals the system is sending. That's it. That's the entire task.

This small act of observation is the first and most critical part of **Step 1 of the Drive Method**. It shifts your perspective from being a participant inside the system to an architect who is observing it. You'll be amazed at the misalignments you suddenly see everywhere. This is the true starting point of motivational design.

Putting It All Together: Anatomy of a Transformation

Once you start seeing the signals, you can begin to design better systems. The following case study illustrates how the full five-step **Drive Method** comes together to solve a complex problem.

Example:

The Client: An engineering company.

- **Step 1: Diagnose the Current Status** The company wanted to improve cross-team collaboration and innovation. However, their primary system for encouraging this was a leaderboard showing who contributed the most documents to a shared database. The audit revealed a clear misalignment: the desired behavior (proactive knowledge-sharing, thoughtful contribution) required **integrated motivation**, but the system was rewarding a frantic, competitive race for volume, which is driven by **external** and **introjected motivation**. Engineers were hoarding insights to post them at the right time, and collaboration was actually decreasing.
- **Step 2: Choose the Right Design Approach** Using the **Behavioral Solution Matrix**, we immediately ruled out explicit, competitive tools like leaderboards, as they would only deepen the motivational gap. The goal was to move from external pressure to integrated purpose. We selected a bundle of more implicit, autonomy-supportive tools: a feedback loop system, social proof mechanics, and a private, gamified mastery dashboard.
- **Step 3: Engineering the Experience** We designed an **IntrinsiQ Performance Journey** to foster intrinsic drive:

- **Curiosity:** We seeded the company's intranet with "unsolved engineering puzzles" e.g. real anomalies from other projects that invited investigation.
- **Interest:** When engineers began exploring these puzzles, they unlocked access to a shared "Insight Threadboard" where they could collaborate on solutions.
- **Positive Externality:** A new "Ripple Feed" quietly showed contributors how their suggestions were being used by other teams, making their impact visible and meaningful.
- **Autonomy:** Engineers could choose how to contribute: by solving unsolved questions, mentoring others, or refining existing solutions. Each path was recognized as equally valuable.
- **Mastery:** Instead of a public leaderboard, each engineer had a private "Mastery Map" that visualized their growing expertise and the complexity of the problems they'd solved.
- **Step 4: Capabilities Required** The design required a new skill from leadership. We trained team leads to facilitate "curiosity conversations" and to give feedback on behavioral signals (e.g., "I noticed you took a risk by sharing that early-stage idea...") rather than just managing output.
- **Step 5: Management System** To make the new system legitimate, we worked with HR to add "Collaborative Impact" as a key indicator in quarterly performance reviews. Progress on the Mastery Map and contributions to the Ripple Feed were now officially recognized and rewarded, bridging the gap between the motivational system and the organizational one.

The result was a profound shift. The frantic race for leaderboard points disappeared, replaced by a culture of genuine problem-solving. The system was no longer a place to perform, but a place to grow

The journey from a 15-minute audit to a full system transformation is challenging but immensely rewarding. It is the real work of modern leadership.

Final Word

The real test of leadership has never been whether people obey. It has always been whether they grow. The organizations that endure are not those that extract the most in the shortest time but those that create environments where people want to keep becoming more.

This book has not been about new tricks to squeeze performance. It has been about a shift in perspective: to see motivation not as fuel you burn, but as energy you cultivate. To see systems not as machines, but as journeys where curiosity, challenge, and mastery compound into something far greater than the sum of their parts.

Every company, every team, every individual stands at the same crossroads. One path promises predictability, control, and the comfort of targets. The other promises uncertainty, growth, and the extraordinary returns that only trust and intrinsic drive can deliver.

The choice is not mine. It is yours. And perhaps, it is ours together.

About the Author

Roman Rackwitz has spent the past two decades exploring one central question: why do people give their best in games, sports, or hobbies, but often hold back in the workplace? His search for answers led him from early experiments with gamification to building one of Europe's longest-standing agencies in the field, and ultimately to developing the Drive Method.

He has worked with organizations across industries, from global corporations to emerging ventures, always with the same focus: creating environments where people commit, not just comply. His thinking combines insights from behavioral economics, evolutionary psychology, and neuroscience with practical experience gained from years of helping teams, leaders, and designers rethink how performance emerges.

Beyond consulting, Roman is a regular lecturer, speaker, and writer on motivation design. He sees his role less as a motivator and more as a translator: turning scientific insights into systems that work in everyday business.

When he is not writing or working with clients, he is most at home experimenting with new ideas, learning from games, and finding better ways to connect human potential with meaningful challenges.

Acknowledgements

To my family, thank you for your patient support, clear orientation, and the steady encouragement that kept me moving through this book. I owe more than words can carry. I am equally grateful to the universities, business schools, and institutions that invited me to lecture while I developed the ideas collected here. Particular mention should be made here of the Institute for Communication & Leadership IKF in Lucerne, Switzerland, and Munich Business School, Germany.

And to the individuals who pushed, questioned, or simply believed at the right moment, your impact is present in every chapter. Thanks for your curiosity, questions, and critique:

Bernardo Letayf

Uwe Müsse

Clemens Lutsch

Simon Schulte

Ricardo Görlich

Ercan Altuğ YILMAZ

Arne Gels

Christoph Deeg

Nicolas Babin

Undine Zumpe

and many more.

List of Figures, and Info Boxes:

Figures

Figure 1: Flow channel

Figure 2: The Drive Method

Figure 3: The Drive Method - Step 1

Figure 4: The Drive Method - Step 2

Figure 5: The Behavioral Solution Matrix™

Figure 6: The Behavioral Solution Matrix™ - Interventions

Figure 7: The Drive Method - Step 3

Figure 8: The IntrinsiQ™ Performance Journey Loop

Figure 9: IntrinsiQ™ Loop - Step 1: Curiosity

Figure 10: IntrinsiQ™ Loop - Step 2: Interest

Figure 11: IntrinsiQ™ Loop - Step 3: Positive Externality

Figure 12: IntrinsiQ™ Loop - Step 4: Autonomy

Figure 13: IntrinsiQ™ Loop - Step 5: Mastery

Figure 14: The Drive Method - Step 4

Figure 15: The Drive Method - Step 5

Info Boxes

Info Box 1: What is Intrinsic Motivation?

Info Box 2: Oxytocin & Vasopressin

Info Box 3: What I Mean by Non-Skinnerian Gamification

Info Box 4: What Are Zero-Sum Activities, and Why Do They Matter?

Info Box 5: The Six Motivation Types

Info Box 6: The IKEA Effect

Info Box 7: Dopamine is about anticipation and pursuit, not just the pleasure of reward

Info Box 8: Explicit vs Implicit Design

Info Box 9: Some well-known behavioral design interventions

Info Box 10: How a tool is placed in a specific quadrant

Info Box 11: Connection to the Self-Determination Theory (SDT)

Further Reading

This book stands on the shoulders of researchers, neuroscientists, and designers who have dedicated their lives to understanding the complex machinery of human motivation. For those who wish to go deeper, the following works provide the foundational science and philosophy behind the frameworks in this book.

Amabile, Teresa & Kramer, Steven. *The Progress Principle: Using Small Wins to Ignite Joy, Engagement, and Creativity at Work.* The definitive exploration of the core idea in **Insight #1**: that making consistent, meaningful progress is the most powerful driver of workplace motivation. This is essential reading for any leader looking to build systems that highlight and celebrate small wins.

Clear, James. *Atomic Habits: An Easy & Proven Way to Build Good Habits & Break Bad Ones.* While my book focuses on designing systems for *others*, Clear's work provides the definitive guide on how behavior change and habits are formed at the *individual* level. His model of "Cue, Craving, Response, Reward" is a practical and powerful lens for understanding the mechanics of any behavioral loop.

Csikszentmihalyi, Mihaly. *Flow: The Psychology of Optimal Experience.* The foundational text on the state of "flow," where a person is fully immersed in an activity with energized focus. Csikszentmihalyi's work is the bedrock for understanding how to design the "meaningful challenges" discussed in **Insight #3**.

Edmondson, Amy C. *The Fearless organization: Creating Psychological Safety in the Workplace for Learning, Innovation, and Growth.* This book is the seminal text on psychological safety. Edmondson provides the research and framework to understand the single most important cultural ingredient for intrinsic motivation to flourish. A system can be perfectly designed, but without the psychological safety for people to experiment, fail, and be vulnerable, it will never reach its full potential.

Eyal, Nir. *Hooked: How to Build Habit-Forming Products.* Eyal introduces the "Hook Model," a four-step process (Trigger, Action, Variable Reward, Investment) that many successful technology products use to create user engagement. His insights into "variable rewards" directly complement our discussion of dopamine's role in driving pursuit and are highly relevant to the design of the **IntrinsiQ Performance Journey**™.

Kahneman, Daniel. *Thinking, Fast and Slow.* For the reader who truly wants a deep dive into the science of decision-making, this is the foundational text. Written by a Nobel laureate, it details the two systems of thought: the fast, intuitive "System 1" and the slow, deliberate "System 2." Understanding this dual-process model provides a profound context for why implicit, "System 1" nudges and explicit, "System 2" instructions (as detailed in your **Behavioral Solution Matrix**™) must be used in different situations.

Koster, Raph. *A Theory of Fun for Game Design.* A seminal work that dismantles the concept of "fun" and reveals it to be another word for learning. Koster's argument that we enjoy mastering new patterns is critical to understanding why **Non-Skinnerian Gamification** is about growth, not gimmicks.

McGonigal, Jane. *Reality Is Broken: Why Games Make Us Better and How They Can Change the World.* McGonigal makes a powerful, optimistic case for applying the principles of game design to solve real-world problems. This book is an excellent resource for showing that game mechanics can foster collaboration, resilience, and even epic meaning.

Pink, Daniel H. *Drive: The Surprising Truth About What Motivates Us.* This book brings the science of motivation to a business audience. Pink masterfully translates the work of Deci and Ryan into a compelling case for focusing on Autonomy, Mastery, and Purpose.

Ryan, Richard M., & Deci, Edward L. *Self-Determination Theory: Basic Psychological Needs in Motivation, Development, and Wellness.* This is the comprehensive academic text on the theory that underpins much of this book.

For the reader who wants to go directly to the source, this work explains the non-negotiable human needs for **autonomy, competence, and relatedness**, which are the building blocks of intrinsic motivation.

Sapolsky, Robert M. *Behave: The Biology of Humans at Our Best and Worst.* A brilliant and exhaustive exploration of why we do what we do, from the neurochemical triggers seconds before an action to the evolutionary pressures that shaped our ancestors. Sapolsky's work provides the deep scientific context for the discussions on **dopamine, oxytocin, and vasopressin**.

Suits, Bernard. The Grasshopper: Games, Life and *Utopia*. A witty and profound philosophical examination of what defines a "game." Suits' classic definition - "the voluntary attempt to overcome unnecessary obstacles" - is a crucial lens for understanding why we are drawn to challenges and why this concept is central to effective gamification design.

Glossary of Key Terms

Amotivation: The lowest level on the spectrum of motivation as described by Self-Determination Theory, representing a complete lack of motivation.

Autonomy: A core psychological need where individuals feel they are the authors of their own actions and can make meaningful choices that shape their journey. It is considered a neurobiological requirement for motivation, not just a management style.

Behavioral Solution Matrix™: A strategic tool used in the Drive Method™ to align the right behavioral design intervention with the specific type of motivation required for a task. It uses two axes: the type of motivation (from amotivation to intrinsic) and the nature of the design (from implicit to explicit).

Coherence: The alignment between an organization's stated values and the actual signals sent by its systems, rituals, and rewards. A lack of coherence creates dissonance and cynicism, while high coherence builds trust and engagement.

Competence: A core psychological need, also referred to as Mastery, where individuals feel effective, capable, and are able to grow their skills.

Dopamine: A key neurochemical linked to motivation. It is not a "pleasure chemical" released upon reward, but rather a "pursuit chemical" that drives anticipation, focus, and goal-directed behavior by signaling that a reward *might* be coming.

Drive Method™: The book's proprietary five-step roadmap for designing and building sustainable motivation systems. The steps are: 1. Current Status, 2. Choosing the Fit, 3. Engineering the Experience, 4. Capabilities Required, and 5. Management System.

Endorphins: Neurochemicals that help individuals push through discomfort and reinforce effort. They are part of the psychological reward for overcoming challenges and are engaged during the Mastery phase of the IntrinsiQ Performance Journey™.

Explicit Design Tools: Motivational interventions that are obvious and visible to the user. They shape behavior through clear rules, structures, and consequences. Examples include checklists, reward programs, and leaderboards.

External Regulation: A type of extrinsic motivation where behavior is controlled by external rewards or the threat of punishment.

Extrinsic Motivation: Motivation driven by external factors, such as money, bonuses, grades, or praise, rather than internal satisfaction from the task itself.

Flow: An optimal state of deep immersion and energized focus in an activity, occurring when the challenge level is perfectly balanced with an individual's skill level. It is characterized by clear goals, immediate feedback, and a sense of effortless effort.

Gamification: The application of game-like principles and mechanics (such as progress, feedback, and exploration) to real-world systems to make them more engaging. The book distinguishes this from the common misconception of simply adding points, badges, and leaderboards.

Implicit Design Tools: Subtle motivational interventions that guide behavior without the user's conscious awareness. They shape action through environmental cues, framing, and friction. Examples include smart defaults, progress bars, and narrative cues.

Identified Motivation: A type of motivation where an individual comes to value a goal and sees it as personally important, even if the activity is not intrinsically enjoyable.

Integrated Motivation: A form of extrinsic motivation where goals and values are fully assimilated into a person's sense of self. It is very close to intrinsic motivation on the motivation spectrum.

Intrinsic Motivation: Motivation that comes from within, where an activity is performed because it is inherently interesting, enjoyable, or meaningful. The activity itself is the reward.

IntrinsiQ Performance Journey™: A five-phase framework for engineering intrinsic motivation. The loop consists of: 1. Curiosity, 2. Interest, 3. Positive Externality, 4. Autonomy, and 5. Mastery.

Introjected Motivation: A type of motivation driven by internal pressures, such as performing an action to avoid guilt, feel worthy, or maintain self-esteem.

KPIs (Key Performance Indicators): Metrics used to measure performance. The book argues that traditional KPIs, often relics of the industrial age, are suited for repetitive tasks but can stifle creativity and innovation when misapplied to complex work.

Mastery: The satisfying feeling of becoming more skilled and competent at a challenging task. It is the emotional payoff in the IntrinsiQ Performance Journey™ and a core psychological need.

Non-Skinnerian Gamification: The book's term for its approach to gamification, which focuses on fostering intrinsic motivation through design rather than relying on the extrinsic reward-and-punishment systems (operant conditioning) associated with B.F. Skinner. It prioritizes autonomy, progress, and meaning over points and prizes.

Oxytocin: A neurochemical that governs trust, social bonding, and connection. It is often called the "cuddle hormone" and is activated when people feel a sense of belonging and see their contributions helping others.

Positive Externality: A phase in the IntrinsiQ Performance Journey™ where an individual sees that their effort has a positive, visible impact on others, the team, or the system, reinforcing their sense of purpose and connection.

Progress Principle: The principle that making visible, meaningful progress in one's work is a primary driver of motivation.

The feeling of being "almost there" is often more motivating than completion itself.

Relatedness: A core psychological need to feel connected to others, to care for and be cared for by others, and to feel a sense of belonging within a group or community.

Second-order effect: The indirect consequences that follow an initial change. They appear after people adapt to the new rules, incentives, or tools. These effects can amplify or undermine the original goal.

Self-Determination Theory (SDT): A major theory of human motivation that posits all humans have three innate psychological needs: Autonomy, Competence, and Relatedness. The theory also describes a spectrum of motivation from amotivation to intrinsic motivation.

Serotonin: A neurochemical linked to feelings of pride, status, and being valued within a group. It contributes to the sense of confidence and significance that comes from achievement and recognition.

The IKEA Effect: A cognitive bias where people place a disproportionately high value on things they have partially created or built themselves. The book applies this to motivation, arguing that people are more engaged in systems they help shape.

Vanity metrics: Surface-level numbers that look impressive but do not reflect meaningful progress or behavior change, for example likes, views, and clicks.

Vasopressin: A neurochemical that plays a key role in loyalty, group defense, and social bonding, particularly through shared challenge and duty. It is crucial for building cohesion in high-pressure situations.

Zero-Sum Activity: An activity or competition where one person's gain directly results in another's loss (e.g., a classic leaderboard). The book warns that this framing can undermine collaboration and demotivate the majority of participants.

Endnotes

1   Progress Principle; Teresa M. Amabile, Steven Kramer

2   Siehe Insight #1

3   Csikszentmihalyi, M. (1990). Flow: The Psychology of Optimal Experience. New York: Harper & Row / Harper Perennial.

4   Pink, D. H. (2009). Drive: The Surprising Truth About What Motivates Us. New York: Riverhead Books.

5   Gallup. (2023). State of the Global Workplace: 2023 Report.

6   Sapolsky, R. M. (2017). Behave: The Biology of Humans at Our Best and Worst. Penguin Press.

7   Huberman, A. (2022). "Tools to Manage Dopamine and Improve Motivation & Drive."

8   Sapolsky, Robert M. (2017). Behave: The Biology of Humans at Our Best and Worst. Penguin Press. ISBN: 978-1594205071

9   Kelly M Dumais (2015), National Library of Medicine: Vasopressin and oxytocin receptor systems in the brain: sex differences and sex-specific regulation of social behavior

10   Amabile, T. M., & Kramer, S. J. (2011). The Progress Principle.

11   Kosfeld et al. (2005)

12   Csikszentmihalyi, M. (1990). Flow: The Psychology of Optimal Experience. New York: Harper & Row. Classic source describing flow and the balance between challenge and skill (the "flow channel").

13   Johannsen, R., et al. (2020)

14   Crockett, M. J., et al. (2010)

15   Ericsson, K. Anders, Michael J. Prietula, and Edward T. Cokely. "The Making of an Expert." Harvard Business Review, July–August 2007

16   Mark, G., Gudith, D., & Klocke, U. (2008). "The Cost of Interrupted Work: More Speed and Stress." Proceedings of the SIGCHI Conference on Human Factors in Computing Systems, 107–110.

17   Dignan, Aaron. (2011). Game Frame: Using Games as a Strategy for Success. Free Press.

18   Deci, E. L., Koestner, R., & Ryan, R. M. (1999). "A Meta-Analytic Review of Experiments Examining the Effects of Extrinsic Rewards on Intrinsic Motivation." Psychological Bulletin, 125(6), 627–668

19 Deci, E. L., Koestner, R., & Ryan, R. M. (1999). "A Meta-Analytic Review of Experiments Examining the Effects of Extrinsic Rewards on Intrinsic Motivation." Psychological Bulletin, 125(6), 627–668.

20 Huberman Lab Podcast, Episode: "Dr. Adam Grant: How to Unlock Your Potential, Motivation & Unique Abilities" (November 27, 2023)

21 Oyserman, D., & Destin, M. (2010). Identity-based motivation: Implications for intervention. The Counseling Psychologist, 38(7), 1001–1043. https://doi.org/10.1177/0011000010374775

22 Hackman, J. R., & Oldham, G. R. (1976). "Motivation through the Design of Work: Test of a Theory." organizational Behavior and Human Performance, 16(2), 250–279.

23 Deci, E. L., & Ryan, R. M. (1985). Intrinsic Motivation and Self-Determination in Human Behavior. New York: Springer.

24 Ryan, Richard M., and Edward L. Deci. 2000. "Self-Determination Theory and the Facilitation of Intrinsic Motivation, Social Development, and Well-Being." American Psychologist 55(1): 68–78.

25 https://selfdeterminationtheory.org/theory/

26 Deci, E. L., & Ryan, R. M. (2000). "The 'What' and 'Why' of Goal Pursuits: Human Needs and the Self-Determination of Behavior." Psychological Inquiry, 11(4), 227–268.

27 Amabile, T. M., & Kramer, S. J. (2011). The Progress Principle: Using Small Wins to Ignite Joy, Engagement, and Creativity at Work. Harvard Business Review Press.

28 Norton, M. I., Mochon, D., & Ariely, D. (2012). The IKEA Effect: When Labor Leads to Love. Journal of Consumer Psychology, 22(3), 453–460. https://doi.org/10.1016/j.jcps.2011.08.002

29 Sapolsky, R. M. (2017). Behave: The Biology of Humans at Our Best and Worst. Penguin Press.

30 Bernard Suits, The Grasshopper: Games, Life and Utopia (1978) 11; Mihaly Csikszentmihalyi

31 Edward L. Deci, "Effects of externally mediated rewards on intrinsic motivation" (1971)

32 Sam Glucksberg (1962), Edward Deci (1971), Lepper, Greene, & Nisbett (1973), Teresa Amabile (1985–1996)

33 Deci, E. L., Koestner, R., & Ryan, R. M. (1999). "A Meta-Analytic Review of Experiments Examining the Effects of Extrinsic Rewards on Intrinsic Motivation." Psychological Bulletin, 125(6), 627–668.

34 Michael I. Norton, Daniel Mochon, and Dan Ariely, "The IKEA Effect: When Labor Leads to Love" (2012).

35 Simons, T. (2002). "The High Cost of Lost Trust: When Employees Don't Believe Managers' Words." Harvard Business Review, 80(9), 18–19.

36 Lazear, Edward, P. 2000. "Performance Pay and Productivity." American Economic Review 90 (5): 1346–1361

37 Kahneman 2011, p. 71, 85

38 Kotler, S., Mannino, M., Kelso, S., & Huskey, R. (2022). "First few seconds for flow: A comprehensive proposal of the neurobiology and neurodynamics of state onset." Neuroscience & Biobehavioral Reviews, 143, 104956.

39 Thaler, R. H., & Sunstein, C. R. (2008). Nudge: Improving Decisions About Health, Wealth, and Happiness. Penguin Books.

www.ingramcontent.com/pod-product-compliance
Lightning Source LLC
Chambersburg PA
CBHW071416210326
41597CB00020B/3522